er

## A 4,000-year walk along the river Alun

Pete Evans

Gwasg Carreg Gwalch

First published in 2017
© Pete Evans / Gwasg Carreg Gwalch

Published by Gwasg Carreg Gwalch,
12 Iard yr Orsaf, Llanrwst, Conwy, LL26 0EH.
tel: 01492 642031 Ffacs: 01492 641502
email: llyfrau@carreg-gwalch.com
website: www.carreg-gwalch.com

ISBN: 978-1-84524-265-7

Cover design:Eleri Owen

Photo/illustration credits:
*Pages 7 and 33* – Eira Evans; *Pages 2, 4, 27, 38, 46, 51, 53, 55 and 69* – Sophia Evans; *Pages 108 and 111* – A. Parsonage

## Acknowledgements

The author is grateful to Sophia, Eira and Sion for assistance and patience, to Flintshire and Denbighshire Countryside and Library services, particularly the knowledgeable and enthusiastic Park Rangers for guidance and enlightenment. Warm thanks also to the Welsh Mills Society for information provided on mills on the Alun and to Ali Parsonage for material on the Caergwrle area, all much appreciated.

*Cover Photo:* Fagl Lane Quarry, adjacent to the river Alun near Hope

1. *Wild garlic at Loggerheads;*
2. *Pentre Mill, Loggerheads;*
*Overleaf: Clapper Bridge*

# Contents

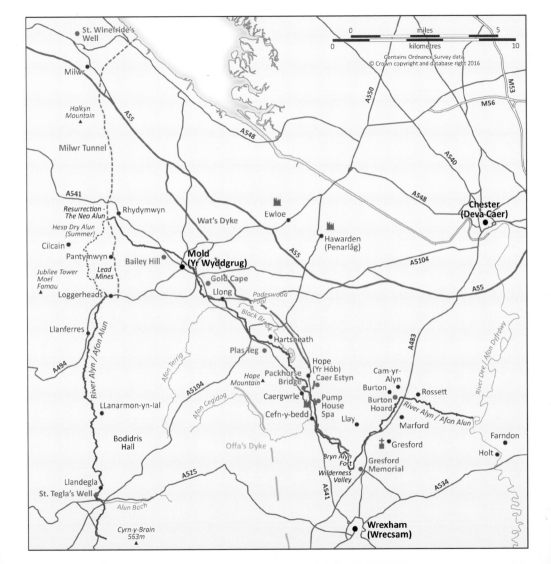

# 1. The Alun River

The Alun is a river of tranquillity, of droughts, floods and trade; fortunes made and lost. At times it doesn't exist at all and yet at the same time it is two rivers!

This ubiquitous river in north-eastern Wales flows quietly for the most part, popping up in short flashes viewed from the car window as we drive past, no plaques or signs mark her start, finish or crossing points – though her name crops up regularly in houses and hills, businesses and schools, a public house and a country park.

This book follows the Alun through landscape and time, from county to county, country to country, language to language, all of which have been fluid entities in their own right in their mayfly-span of comparative existence.

The alpha village of Llandegla sets the tone for the journey ahead with its bible pillow spell and troublesome poltergeist; onwards the Alun flows through farmlands where she once powered corn mills, into the industrial revolution and the Loggerheads mining area where she simultaneously aided and thwarted the extraction of lead ore and her waters disappear underground for a large part of the year.

At Rhydymwyn the Alun is resurrected, she flows once more; this is not the only transformation which has occurred here, the valley works was once a production site for WMD, it is now reborn into a thriving nature reserve. A short distance downstream a battle was fought which was won in a more sedate manner, with chants not weapons.

At Mold, her biggest town, the creativity theme continues, it being the hometown of the father of the Welsh novel and the resting place of the father of British landscape painting. The jewel of the Alun was found here on her banks, the internationally significant Bronze Age Mold Cape, the largest piece of prehistoric gold work ever found in Britain.

Onwards the corridor of stories flows to the historic villages of Caergwrle and Hope. Here there are tales of a historic national power struggle which resulted in the first nobleman on these isles being hung, drawn and quartered.

*Fairy Glen*

Through a wilderness valley, past Gresford with her tragic coal mining past and magnificent All Saints church where pilgrims flocked for hundreds of years to make offerings to a long forgotten artefact, and finally to soft lush plains, the omega village of Rossett with her taxing mills, to complete the odyssey and quietly slip into the waters of the Dee.

The Alun is an esoteric river. Join me as I journey the length of this little river with a very big history, revealing her many tales and secrets.

# 2. The Awakening

*"In a morning's stroll along the banks of the Alun, a beautiful little stream which flows down from the Welsh hills and throws itself into the Dee"*

*Washington Irving*

I pull out my map, pinpoint our location, and run my finger along the thin blue line until I come to the words "R.Alyn, Afon Alun."

I have lived in the north-eastern Welsh borderlands for three and a half decades, on and off, during which time the river Alun has made fleeting appearances in my semi-consciousness. I didn't have a whole heap of definitive knowledge about it; I didn't really know where it started or finished. I was aware of it in the Mold area flowing from the general direction of Rhydymwyn and I imagined its higher reaches continuing on the same axis, from the direction of Denbigh. I knew it went downstream through Hope and Caergwrle but the route thereafter was a bit of a mystery. This chance meeting was unexpected in its beauty and wildness. I never thought the little Alun could be so majestic.

So many questions: where did the Alun go from here? A quick check of my map showed it flowing past Gresford, through Rossett, and on into the river Dee, downstream from Holt and Farndon. With one half of the jigsaw put in place, I put digit to paper and followed the route upstream as far as Rhydymwyn – no real shocks here, but there the trail ran cold, for the moment anyway, as that's as far as the map I was carrying covered.

And so it was that a cool, clear, blue-skied November morning's "let's get the train to Wrexham and walk back along Wat's Dyke" delivered to us one of life's curved balls, a beautiful tangent – an interest, a curiosity and an affinity with the river Alun was born which has endured, nay flourished and enriched, through many a season.

Topographically uplifted, we continued on our way with renewed vigour, determined to enjoy the remaining section of Wat's Dyke and whatever other treats that lay ahead of us.

A decision was made to check out the full route of the Alun from the book-

*Approaching Loggerheads*

strewn comfort of the living room – to satisfy a new-born geographical curiosity.

As it transpired, the Wat's Dyke peregrination took longer than intended. Not that there was a detailed plan. There was a start point: Wrexham; an end point: our house, and an indeterminate time twixt the two. Progress was at first steady rather than swift; the pause to soak in the Shangri-La find of Wilderness Valley, as it is aptly named, slowed our journey and then darkness rudely intervened, as the aromas of the east carried teasingly across the river to two tired and hungry travellers.....

The Alun research slipped to the following morning.

# 3. Meandering One

So, upstream to Rhydymwyn I was reasonably familiar with. Thereafter the Alun veered towards Cilcain; unexpected, though not a shock. But then it turned south to Loggerheads, which to me was a revelation. In the 1980s I lived at nearby Gwernymynydd and frequently walked by the river in the Loggerheads area. I had always thought this river was called "the Leete." My dictionary defines a leat thus: an open watercourse connected to a mill, more on this later.

Tracing the route backwards past Llanferres, the river narrows to a thin blue line; it is finally identified as the Alun just before Llanarmon-yn-Ial.

The route is therefore... interesting. From its source it heads north; with a north-easterly kink near Cilcain, towards its logical and ultimate end point in the Dee estuary, but Halkyn Mountain, like a burly nightclub bouncer, refuses entry. Time-soaked geology deflects the little Alun south-eastward, kissing the suburbs of Wrexham at the spectacular chicane that is Wilderness Valley. Here the Alun does an about-turn from south briefly back to north again, before entering a lush valley after Gresford, finishing off with an easterly flurry into the Dee. Top marks to the spatially aware Welshman who gave this tortuous river its name. (Alun in Welsh means "*meandering one*").

This book  is a record of findings, discoveries, experiences, epiphanies of nature and self, wet feet, wrong turnings and blue, blue skies. The wild inaccuracies, rumour and conjecture contained within it are deliberate prompts to stimulate the reader into research, bar-room discussions or eyebrow raising-exercises. My plan was to follow, as closely as possible, the route of the river with map in hand.

Optional advice: if these scribbles kindle an interest to walk any of the Alun, wear comfortable footwear; dress according to season, personal taste and morality; leave only footprints; obtain sustenance on the way; support village life. Travel like a pilgrim, if you see an interesting looking diversion, take it.

*Crisp winter morning near Llanferres*

# 4. Sources, Spells and Ghosts

And so it came to pass that on a chilly damp November morning, we set off for Llanarmon-yn-Iâl. The previous night I had concluded my fireside research with the conviction that the Alun started in a boggy morass to the south of Llanarmon, this being, close enough for cash, the start of the Alun.

As we approached Llanarmon, however, at the outskirts of the village we crossed the road bridge by the cave, pausing to see the Alun disappearing below us, full, fast and true. It was clear I couldn't dismiss the source of the river as been "Llanarmon-ish."

We continued onward, along criss-crossing lanes, taking one of them by mistake which required a U-turn at a dead end, witnessed by some concerned-looking farm folk. We arrived at Llandegla at a bridge at the bottom of a hill, the river was again boisterous; clearly there was still some way to go to the source. The water was tinted brown, the heavy rains having flushed in particles of peat. (I was once told by a fisherman that salmon can detect these traces of peat in the estuaries and know that the rivers are high enough for them to start their epic ascents).

We parked up near an attractive church, across the road from a schoolhouse, and a memorial hall where the good people of the village were setting up a bazaar. I have travelled through the lights at Llandegla junction at the other end of the village many times, usually in a rush, completely oblivious to Llandegla's charm. We walked past quaint cottages, (including the mole catcher's) to the chirpy post office, (sadly closed on a subsequent visit, but I am much pleased to relate that a warm and welcoming community run shop/cafe is now open in the old schoolhouse). The ladies of the village inside confirmed that the river at the bottom of the hill was indeed the Alun, but when pressed on its source were less sure and offered differing views "Llanferres?" and "It goes up past the Crown."

At the centre of the village, a tourist information board proclaims; "the river

Alun which flows through Llandegla is a special feature of the AONB (Area of Outstanding Natural Beauty). This river is home to both otter and water vole." A short pause: otter – I've never seen one in the wild. Nocturnal, secretive; I wonder what my chances are. Water vole – I've never knowingly seen one of those either, not unless I've mistaken one for a rat (of which I've seen lots).

The board goes on to give details of the Offa's Dyke path which goes through the village. Signposts give Chepstow as being 148 miles to the south, while Prestatyn is a more manageable 29 to the north. Llandegla was located on one of the main drovers' roads from North Wales to the markets at Wrexham, Chester and beyond. There were up to 16 inns in the village and four fairs a year which catered to this trade. It wasn't just cattle that were driven – some of the inns had holes/chimneys built into their walls for tarring the feet of geese to withstand the journey. The Alun and the trade routes across North Wales meet up many times on their ways east.

We walked past the church, back along the road by which we entered the village

*St Tegla's well*

and over the bridge from where a riverside path was signed "St Tegla's well".

Who can resist such a sign? We were drawn to the opposite bank over a wooden bridge to the perfectly kept well which sat next to two old moss-covered trees. A layer of leaves coated the floor of the flat river bank; votive ribbons were tied here and there onto thin shoots which radiated upward.

Just a few yards into our journey on the very first day we were delivered the first of many delicious treats, which whetted the appetite for the way ahead. A fabulously artistic information board explained:

"This small well was once renowned across North Wales for its healing properties. It reputedly cured epilepsy, known locally as *Clwyf Tecla*.

Sufferers hoping for a cure undertook an elaborate ritual after sunset. 'Wash your limbs in the well and make an offering of four pence. Walk three times around the well and then the church carrying a chicken whilst reciting the Lord's Prayer. Enter the church and lie under the communion table with the bible under your head and rest there until daybreak. Depart leaving the chicken and sixpence.'

If the chicken died the epileptic was cured. Sufferers may have assisted the bird's death by pricking it with pins! Long silver pins have been found in the well."

The power of superstition was clearly strong when the ritual was performed. It must have been a desperate pre-NHS act by poor people hoping for a cure. I do not recall any of Jesus' miracles requiring an exchange of cash or poultry. I suspect that before the church discouraged the practise in the nineteenth century, the local vicar may have lived in some comfort, possibly enjoying an occasional good roast.

If that weren't enough folklore for this first village on the Alun, it is said that under the bridge which carries the Llanarmon road an unusual box lies buried, which, if I were to stumble upon it, I would resist any temptation to open. The story goes that at the nearby Rectory, a poltergeist was making the lives of its occupants a misery. A Reverend was asked to exorcise the ghost, which took many forms. He managed to change it into a bluebottle which he contained in a small box and placed under a stone below the bridge. The ghost protested, and the Reverend relented, allowing it to be set free when the height of a nearby tree reached the parapet of the bridge. For many years the villagers cut back the branches of the tree, thereby keeping the ghost secure in the box. This practice, however, has long since ceased...better tread carefully here.

Continuing upstream, the path took us to the A525, under which the Alun passes. We peered over the road-side wall and were presented with a conundrum – two streams converge by the bridge. This time we were better prepared, having about us a map borrowed from Mold Library – not just any map – an active map, for all extremes: a sort of a plastic-covered super-tough affair. The slightly smaller branch, running from the direction of Bwlchgwyn, was not identified; we followed the larger flow, again not tagged, toward Cyrn-y-Brain (*the cairns of the crows*).

It soon became apparent that the valley floor here was like a giant sponge.

Tributaries converged from all directions, springs gurgled up effervescent water from the surrounding hills. The torrential overnight rain was being collected here and despatched downstream.

We followed the path over a footbridge which bore a moss-covered inscription "Denbighshire County Council 1950". The river turned south-west, diminishing in strength and dividing into many tributaries. My map showed capillary-like blue lines networking through the landscape.

The whole area is the source of the Alun; it would be possible and no doubt enjoyable to trace it to a single trickle, but which one? And does it really matter? Does everything have to be identified exactly? This way some mystery remains. Well, that was my excuse anyway. I concluded that the Alun is born from a myriad of sources in this upland water bowl before repairing to the village.

At St Tegla's church a lady was busy setting up for the Sunday remembrance service. She was chatty and welcoming; she kindly gave us leaflets and a short guided tour.

The church is most famous for its

*St Tegla's church*

*Bod Idris Hall near Llandegla*

handsome candelabra, surmounted with the figure of the Virgin Mary. It is reputed to have come from Valle Crucis Abbey near Llangollen at the time of the Dissolution. A place of worship is thought to have existed on this site, close to the river Alun, since the seventh century.

We told the lady of our walk to the well and the healing ritual. I asked about the communion table mentioned there which people used to spend the night below – apparently the granting of access to the well and its renovation are recent events and she was unaware of the ritual.

When we mentioned our aim of following the Alun, she helpfully pointed out the Offa's Dyke path which fringes the church and follows the river downstream, before branching off up the Clwydian range.

We have visited Llandegla several times since. It is one of those places that just make us feel good.

One of these visits was to investigate the mill, which we never noticed on our first visit, and the reason we had not spotted it soon became apparent. The information board in the village centre has a photo and the statement "milling was carried out here from the 16th century. The mill shown here was demolished in the 1950's but Bryn Dŵr; the miller's cottage still remains."

The miller's cottage is close to our old friend St Tegla's Well. The corn mill stood on the lawn which leads down to the river. I looked for traces of the mill race but failed to see anything.

"Llandegla then and now" contains several photos of "St Thomas's Mill". It also has the previously mentioned photo which shows the upstream side of the mill with its 'pitch-back' wheel where the flow of water would have arrived and then exited on the same side of the building. It dates the photos at 1898 and identifies the miller in the photo as William Davies – the last person to fulfil this role. He is buried in the mill end of the churchyard 'to keep an eye on his property.' A photo from the downstream or ghost-bridge end shows an 'overshot' wheel carrying the water over the wheel so that the water exited on the opposite side to the incoming flow. This would have meant the wheels turned in opposite directions – an unusual arrangement.

On this particular visit we noticed two very funky camping pods in the grounds of the cottage. This was too good to resist, we made enquiries and some weeks later engaged in a family outing whereby we walked from Mold to Llandegla (mostly along the Clwydian Way) and stayed overnight in the very comfortable pods. (I told Sophia the tale of the ghost under the bridge *after* our stay).To be on the Alun at sun-rise, the sweetest time of day, in a light mist, birds calling, near the healing well, perfect.

*The duelling staircase at Bod Idris, built in the 16th century, it had uneven treads to cause unwelcome swordsmen to lose their balance*

# 5. River of Saints

I left Llandegla in the parish of St Tegla and headed for Llanarmon in the parish of St Garmon, alone this time, taking deep breaths of the rarefied air.

The going was tough. Dollops of creamy mud clung to my wellies. Every step was a big effort. Physically tiring but mentally rejuvenating, the path was free of distraction, there was no entrance fee, no password or PIN required. The ground below my feet was gloriously disinterested in my mother's maiden name or my favourite film.

This was a spacious high-skied, time-bending landscape, a million miles from any city. I half expected Owain Glyndŵr himself to be around the next bend. The area felt old, old, without even a modern farmhouse or barn conversion to bring me back to the present.

The wind rose, clouds gathered, rain started to fall. I was being buffeted by squally gusts of immense strength, feeling like a character in one of those portentous old paintings. A vague memory popped up of someone famous being killed by a falling branch as he walked through Hyde Park.

Downstream, the day calmed and the earth music quietened, sweet pure air filled my lungs. Footpaths and lanes cut across the Alun as it flowed toward Llanarmon. I followed a bridleway up the limestone escarpment, intending to take the first available left turn back towards the river. The path drew me in, tree-lined, leaf-filled with rough limestone chunks, some completely shrouded in moss, a road without cars. I found myself high above the valley floor with four squawking buzzards for company.

I could almost glimpse drovers, miners and pilgrims on the hazy distant paths. Laurie Lee, Patrick Leigh Fermor, George Borrow, Nicholas Crane, and Forest Gump formed a posse around me as I walked.

I wandered further from the river in a kind of daydream, along a ding-dong beautiful hill. I came to a caravan park and golf course secreted away among the limestone hollows, unseen. I paused to absorb the views these lucky people awake to. The hills, the peace, the solitude were all mine, with not a soul about. The Clwydian range ran parallel on my left, rounded shoulder to shoulder under clear blue skies. When I think of the Clwydians, I sometimes envisage the transmitting stations at Moel y Parc and Cyrn y Brain as giant goal posts, with Benlli Gawr the goalkeeper waiting for a penalty to be taken from Cader Idris. I am a small speck up here. With so much headspace, proportions are quantified, thoughts are untangled, and dilemmas are resolved or simply float off on the breeze.

The path onward was poorly blazed. Stiles were completely overgrown, clearly not often walked. Some sections looked as if they had been completely forgotten, to be discovered by some future generation. I avoided angry-looking cows in a feeding frenzy, by skirting around some trees and over some steps, into a farmyard. I walked past a large building containing all manner of trucks and tractors, in front of which a group of farmers were chatting. I waved hello; they turned but didn't respond – bad day at the market? I emerged on a road and checked my map; I had overshot big time. Not only had I missed the Alun; I had missed Llanarmon. I had not been concentrating on my core activity, as they say, but sometimes it is nice to deviate

from a plan and let your senses lead you. I was on the Graianrhyd road about a mile past Llanarmon. I put one foot in front of the other, and soon enough I was on the village outskirts. I crossed the bridge over the Alun, the cave to my right and the mound of Tomen y Faerdre to my left.

The cave is large and looks big enough for habitation from this distance: indeed signs of Neolithic habitation have been found here. The way these islands are filling up, it won't be long before it is occupied once again. Tomen y Faerdre is a motte dating back to the eleventh century, built by the lords of Ial and makes for quite an entrance to a village. It beats the usual boarded-up pub and, if you're lucky, all the quirky shops which once existed that are now squeezed into the confines of one convenience store.

Llanarmon Mill sits close to the bridge. It was named after St Garmon by the current owner, who kindly showed me around. The gable end nearest the road carries an inscription from 1830. This is the date of refurbishment following a fire. Inside a beam gives a date of 1749.

To the rear of the three-story building is the ground floor of a much older part of the mill thought to be eight or nine hundred years old. A water wheel was located at the gable end of this much older section; this was a bucket type wheel which was fed from a pond located to the south of the building. A tail race returned the water the short distance to the Alun via a tunnel. The mill is last thought to have been used to produce animal feed during the war.

The 900m long mill race passed through working fields, its channel now returned to the soil, no longer visible save for the odd high and dry sluice gate.

Up the rise toward the church, a solid stone house stands tall on the corner. From the hill it looks like a skyscraper. The wooden gate at the front incorporates a ships wheel. I seem to remember from somewhere that a ship's captain may have lived here?

I went through the churchyard. The church occupies the whole of the heart of the village, and everything else radiates from it, in the manner of early Celtic settlements. The notice board in the porch testifies it is still at the core of village life. The door is locked (a phone number is displayed, and visits can be arranged) but through the keyhole I see richly coloured windows, but can't quite see the sister candelabra to the one at Llandegla.

I go out through the church gates. When I pull them shut behind me, there is a "no parking" notice attached. There is space for only the smallest of cars, but when I look closer it says: "do not tie your horse here." My kind of place...

A notice board informs the Raven dates from 1722 – the only surviving pub in the area. The parishioners rose to over 2,000 in the 1800's on the back of lead mining, quarrying and droving. Where I walked earlier I viewed a large quarry eating into the hillside. Quarrying still goes on, albeit highly mechanised and requiring less labour. A bus passed containing only a lonely driver. It turned and headed off, still empty. I checked the opening times at the Raven, the door opened and a lady came out. "Its fish and chips Friday" she cheerfully informed me, "Fish fresh from Fleetwood this morning". She told me it was a community-run pub now, having been closed and earmarked for

*1. Llanarmon church;*
*2. Clwydian hills - Moel Arthur;*
*3. Valle Crucis*

"development". What a crime that would have been. I remembered my first visit here over 30 years ago. A friend had said: "sit on the bench in the old fireplace and open the little door in the wall." So in I went, saw the fireplace, settled down, found the door and opened it. An alcove contained a sheep's skull with two table-tennis balls for eyes, complete with red veins painted on. As the door opened, it operated a micro-switch, which lit up the eyes. Happy days... I'm daydreaming again.

I found energy-replacing, warm sweet coffee at the post office which was in keeping with the rest of the village. It had a huge old fireplace, a creaking wooden door and service with a genuine smile.

People stopped off to buy supplies, invariably pausing for a chat. A lady trotted past on a horse. I monitored her, preparing to perform a citizen's arrest if she transgressed the "no parking at the church gate ruling" – doing my bit for the community.

Refreshed, I decided I had not really achieved what I set off to do today, i.e. follow the Alun. I had walked for hours and had an altogether lovely time, but my interaction with the river had been fleeting to say the least. There was about an hour left until the sun set so I headed back over the bridge and turned past Tomen y Faerdre – it must have been quite a pad back in its day. I slipped and slid along a very muddy track up on to the brow of a hill, which had fantastic views back to the village with Moel Famau in the background. The map showed the path had a 90-degree right turn, but, as seems to be the way of these things, I missed it and ended up traipsing far and wide through sodden fields and hawthorn thickets to get to the Alun. When I got there my spirit soon lifted. An ancient clapper bridge eased me over the water flow, its rough cut heavy stone slabs supported on a central pier. Foot-worn and moss-covered, it looked like it had been there for centuries. On the valley floor the sun had set and it was getting chilly. However, this seemed to me a likely spot and an auspicious time to view any shy wildlife. I progressed slowly with my eyes trained on the river.

I came to a narrow road bridge, towards which a farmer was reversing a trailer, temporarily blocking the way. He jumped out and headed towards me. "Have you got a minute?" he asked. He had a flock of sheep which needed repatriating to an adjacent field, and would appreciate it if I could stand in the road a minute blocking the way so that they did not scatter. He opened the trailer; they charged toward me, saw me in the fading light and then paused. He shooed them on, I stood arms outstretched, map in hand, camera around neck, wearing my hand-painted festival wellies and they complied. "You looked like a real farmer there," he smiled.

I asked if he had ever seen otters in the river. "Never" he replied, nor mink, although there is one shown on a Llanarmon website. He went on to say that he was against re-introduction of otters. I queried this – 'they' are trying to introduce them and have built hides further upstream (I didn't recall seeing them. I guess by their nature they are hidden, or maybe I was day-dreaming again). He thinks they will eat birds' eggs, for example those of the curlew (*gylfinir*) – an already dwindling species. This probably was not the time to bring up the legend of the curlew which rescued a book dropped into a river by St Beuno and laid it on a stone to dry. The saint was so grateful he prayed that God would protect the bird, and so, to this day nobody knows where

*Winter damage at the clapper bridge*

the curlew nests.... with the possible exception of otters.

'They' blame farmers for the decline – "but we've been here five generations." When he raised his concerns he was told: "wait until we start on the beavers!"

Tawny owls called from across the valley, Bats flew low above me as I walked slowly, just fast enough to keep the chill off. I didn't want this to end, it felt so right; I enjoyed every deliciously slow step of my return.

I later went back to the Raven, which

was doing a brisk trade in the Fleetwood-supplied fish with chips and delicious-looking foamy beers. The large fireplace to the right of the entrance has its Welsh name "*Y Gigfran*" inscribed into the heavy wooden mantelpiece. A couple of farmers in muddy wellies were enjoying a pint and a chat. When they left, a few curls of dried mud were instantly swept up off the floor by the staff. A declaration on the wall stated the aims and values of the managing community group. I sincerely hope the Raven goes from strength to strength. It would be a crying shame to lose it.

As I left a couple of youngsters were being pelted with wet sponges in the beer garden – not a return to the days of medieval stocks, but a community fund-raiser for Children in Need.

As with Llandegla, so it is with Llanarmon; I now visit whenever I can.

I returned on another day, to the stretch prior to Llanarmon. There was a reason for this: the Welsh Mills Society had kindly supplied me with a list of mills on the Alun and on that list was an entry which read "Creigiog Mill." It was a particularly lovely stretch of water, so I found myself walking down a country lane in the general area of the mill when I came across a man chatting to a lady at the entrance to a field.

The lady, seeing me, broke off her conversation with a "you must be lost." Clearly I was off the beaten path again. "Not quite; I'm looking for Creigiog Mill"

"Ah, you'll be after me then," she said, bade goodbye to her acquaintance and off

*Creigiog Mill*

we went, retracing my steps along one lane, then branching off down another to the delightful Creigiog Mill.

I was treated to a totally unexpected guided tour and history of the mill by the son of the owner. Now, I have a habit of drifting off the trodden path, usually thanks to my bad map-reading, but sometimes through curiosity, so at the outset of this journey I was expecting an occasional "get off my land!" And yet here I found myself, blundering about one minute, the next being invited into someone's home.

It was built in 1575 and is thought to have been in use until the 1920s, from when it fell into a derelict state. An inscription in the fireplace gives the date of rebuilding as 1936. The restoration was carried out by the Dixon Bates family of Chester, who holidayed here for the following 15 years, before selling to the de Kuiper family, who spent their summers here.

The path of the 760m mill race can be clearly traced running parallel to the Alun. A 90-degree bend would have delivered water to the wheel at the southern gable end. A round window here gives the position of its shaft, the vertical drive shaft remains next to the staircase. An old grinding stone still lies in the garden, while a separate grain store has a floor pit in which a fire would have been lit to dry the grain.

Creigiog is mentioned on a notice board in Llanarmon as follows:

"The village had 2 mills by the river Alyn, Creigiog to the south and Garmon closer to the village; records mention a mill on this site in 1315. It is thought that Garmon and Creigiog, along with several other mills along the river, ground corn for Valle Crucis abbey near Llangollen."

# 6. To the River Thief

On a cold, frosty morning I departed from Llanarmon. Locals were constructing a lean-to shelter at the side of the Raven. The sound of hammers on nails filled my ears. It felt in some ways like a frontier outpost, the overshadowing hills waiting for an influx of gold miners.

Three buzzards circled overhead, I heard the flow of the Alun and cockerels crowing nearby. I passed a caravan site, crossed an ancient limestone bridge over the cold river and surprised a heron.

The earth was solid below my feet; I savoured every footstep, from the first touch of the heel to the spring forward from the toes. My mind blissfully free of past events, trivia and things yet to occur, I made a slight detour to Pistyll Gwyn quarry. The term *Pistyll* gave me a glow of anticipation – I expected to see a waterfall nearby, but found none. *Pistyll* can mean a spout of water (as in spring) as well as a cataract or waterfall. In this case the spring was the winner. The quarry is no longer in production and a public footpath threads through its silent workings. A board gives a history of the quarry – including its part in the construction of the WW2 US airbase at Queensferry (Sealand).

I returned to the river following it as closely as I could through thick woods, slip-sliding in the mud and crossing the flow on precariously balanced, moss-covered fallen trees.

Gradually, and not too soon, the landscape opened up into a wide valley along which the Alun gently meanders through supine curves, so much so, that oxbow lakes could actually form here. They haven't, though; the river doesn't quite manage to break through the remaining bank, so that particular geography lesson can stay in the "pending use" area of my brain, along with differential equations and Flemings Left-hand rule. I sometimes wish I could have a clear-out of this extraneous knowledge, to make space for the important stuff I keep forgetting.

A pair of dippers charged towards me, clocked me, then u-turned, like characters in a Disney animation. There was lots of submerged weed on this stretch, good for trout. A white-walled farm sat high on a hill like a hacienda, overlooking the valley. Traffic rushed past on the Mold – Ruthin road, no doubt full of bags of Christmas goodies.

At Plymog (the starting point for many a fine walk) my map showed a ford. This has been superseded by a bridge and there is also a pedestrian crossing which carries a footpath to a host of wonderful locations. A splendid notice board at the nearby lay-by is headed: "gentle exploration brings its own rewards" – my wavelength exactly. It goes on to describe Bryn Alyn as an "international treasure" owing to its limestone pavements – treasure indeed; there should be an "x" on the map. A tributary enters the Alun at this point, which is well worth following for its short distance. My map showed simply 'spr'.

This is wonderfully understated. A series of stepping stones leads to the "Seven Springs" in a cleft in the valley wall below Bryn Alyn. I counted four springs bubbling away in close proximity, but it is easy to imagine another three nearby after a good spell of the wet stuff.

Each spring was a series of mini volcanoes, hypnotically erupting dancing flecks of near-white limestone in crystal clear circles scoured into the mud-caked pebble floor.

It is a gorgeous, benevolent spot. With a touch of undergrowth trimming and sympathetic stonework, it could be truly magical. If history had dealt another hand, perhaps if a saint had settled here, a healing miracle had been performed or even a bottling works set up to capture the pure waters, it could have been quite different. I am glad it has not been developed in any way. The buzzards circling overhead today probably view pretty much the same scene that would have existed a thousand years ago. Some suitable titivation, in harmony with the surroundings, would be the icing on the cake.

*Dipper*

The path continues past an old quarry and kiln to a signpost offering the double delights of the bare summit of Bryn Alyn and the *bendigedig* views there from it, or the contrasting, shaded walk to Maeshafn via Big Covert woods.

The left hand option on the signpost leads to Big Covert cave which is mentioned in the 'explore Maeshafn' booklet as an important archaeological site where Romano-Celtic and Bronze Age finds have been made. There are other caves in the wood which are also archaeologically significant. The reason I know this is that when I was up there one day looking for what I thought was *the* cave I stopped to check my map at a crossroads of footpaths. I looked up and a man was approaching from three o' clock. He not only knew where it was but had actually assisted in the excavation of another cave (named Lynx after a mandible discovered therein). We walked on together and he was a mine (no pun intended) of information on local history. A convivial half-hour was spent at the opening of Big Covert cave discussing caves, potholing, mining and the like. Ah serendipity!

Back at the river, I approached Llanferres which sits on a promontory above a marshy area stretching below her to the river. An improvised child's swing showed simple pleasures still being enjoyed here. The fresh, pure untainted air and clear views of rolling hills slowed up my steps here, in harmony and balance with the surroundings. The sun set early in the shadow of the mountains, bequeathing a crisp dark blue sky.

I crossed the road, following the riverside path, the light through the dense trees faded; flashes of grey were ghostly squirrels. Bad light stopped play.

I walked back along the noisy road toward Llanarmon, arriving at Llanferres where I read the excellent notice boards in the modern un-vandalised bus shelter with my weak-battery torch. The Maeshafn lead mines employed over 400 men at their peak. "Pont y Mwynwr", the Miner's Bridge, at Erw Olchfa was built for miners from Llanferres.

By the time I got to the church it was dark. I returned on another day to view its solid stonework. Easy to imagine the hands of miners using their skills to lay stone upon stone rather than extracting ore from the possessive arms of the Earth.

*Maeshafn lead mine*

*Peacock Butterfly*

This is a sanctuary in a hustle-bustle world; modern roads by-pass these treasures.

In the morning I resumed at Miners' Bridge. The light painted the scenery in more welcoming colours, Blue tits, finches and sparrows skipped across the river from hedge to hedge. On the opposite bank, smoke issued from Erw Olchfa cottage.

Erw means acre, while Olchfa derives from golchi (to wash). This may be the spot referred to in "The Lead Mills of the Alyn Valley" by C.J. Williams where he mentions a dispute over ownership of mining rights in 1734-5 leading to ore being carried to "the river Alyn near Llanferres Bridge to be washed".

A dipper landed on a mossy boulder at the water's edge, his white bib giving him away as he bobbed up and down, acknowledging he had seen me. The dipper is a song bird, uniquely evolved for an aquatic life; to dive for insects and small fish on the river bed, just the right size to give enough strength to withstand the fast flowing upland waters it favours. As well as the "zit-zit" alarm call the dipper has a loud thrush-like song which can be heard above cascading water.

The path here lies twixt the river and the gardens of an enchanting house. Further along, the Welsh name of this area (Coed y Pistyll) becomes apparent as the noise of white water floats up through the trees. I have my white water! As the water flow got faster, I did the opposite. I slowed my pace over the uneven terrain, both for safe passage and to allow time to appreciate the view. I grounded each step carefully, a new rhythm to suit the new landscape.

The river here is partially walled. The remains of the lead works' mill sit on the east bank. In contrast with the corn mills upstream, this was a large solid industrial mill; two separate leats supplied the water over aqueducts and one of the weirs was located well upstream near Llanferres. The lead ore, meanwhile, would have been brought in along a tramway from the Maes-y-safn lead mine, which was worked from the seventeenth century up to 1907. The substantial mill must have needed a large investment in time, effort and money. Its Inca-like stonework is now collapsing, being reclaimed by nature.

In springtime, the smell of ramsons – wild garlic – fills the air here. Their odour identifies them before they come into view, covering the floor of the wood in a carpet of green, speckled with delicate white flowers. As well as the ransoms, this area puts on an incredible display of bluebells. It is easy to see why this is known locally as Fairy Glen.

Just past the old mill, on the opposite bank in front of a bridge, is the first indication and explanation into something which has puzzled me since my dalliance with the Alun began.

A square of dressed stones lying submerged near the edge of the river are the remains of an old well. But why would anyone sink a well in a riverbed?

Thus far the Alun has meandered along through fairly flat countryside, increasing in size, and accumulating a good flow with a width of some 20 feet and a fair old depth in places in rough proportion to the addition of its many tributaries. So why was it that on our way here on this day we

*A well – in the riverbed*

drove past the Alun just outside Mold, several miles downstream, and the flow at a glance seemed to be about half of what we could now see in front of us?

The answer lies in geology. Here the Alun is interrupted by a ridge of limestone which not only diverts its course, adding to its wonderfully circuitous route and well-earned name, but because the limestone is also porous, this thirsty ridge also robs the Alun of its flow through a series of sink holes, diminishing its downstream flow considerably.

And so it was that in the absence of piped water to quench the thirst of the parched miners, and general populace, a well was sunk in the riverbed. It is hard to visualise this on a spring day with the Alun fully replenished, but the river here can become non-existent in summer.

Just before Loggerheads stands Llanferres Mill. Dating from the eighteenth century it once ground corn. A water wheel is still visible; this would have been fed from one of the many weirs along this stretch. The demands on the Alun were high in this area, a succession of weirs siphoning off water for all manner of uses.

*Cascade wood*

*Resurrection River*

# 7. At Loggerheads

In the early eighties I was lucky enough to share a house in nearby Gwernymynydd. If I found my college studies were too taxing – my fuzzy head swimming with calculus or fluid dynamics, I would take a stroll down the hill. A right turn would take me into the park; a left would lead to the Loggerheads Inn: not a bad choice of options for the solving of problems or simply forgetting them.

I have a memory of a winter's afternoon, sat up on the cliff, snow all around, Moel Famau pin-sharp in the cold air. Below I see just an occasional car, weaving an unsteady route along the road below, struggling for traction to reach the safety and warmth of home. On this sunny afternoon there are no such problems. The area around the visitor centre is busy, families play football, couples canoodle and walk their dogs, and cyclists and hikers rest and refresh at the excellent Caffi Florence. It's how a Sunday should be. The area is well managed, clean and inviting.

It wasn't always such a scene of laid-back recreation. Lead mining in Flintshire goes back to Roman times. At Loggerheads, lead was extracted commercially for hundreds of years until the mines closed in the 1870s.

The valuable ore held within the rocks below our feet was inevitably highly contested and left its mark not only on the landscape but also in the very name of this place.

In 1763 following a lengthy legal impasse over mineral rights in which the Lords of Mold (Flintshire) prevailed over the Grosvenor Estate (Llanferres/Denbighshire), a monument was erected over the spot adjudged to be the boundary

*Moel Famau summit*

stone – "Carreg Carn March Arthur" (*the stone of the hoof of Arthur's horse*). The hoof print therein is said to have been made by Arthur's horse as he landed after jumping from the top of Moel Famau. The stone can be seen on the left-hand side, going up the hill from Loggerheads towards Mold. It is located beneath the dressed stone arch of the monument. The inscription on the plaque reads:

*The Stone underneath this Arch*
***CARREG CARN MARCH ARTHUR***
*was adjudged to be the Boundary of the*
*Parish and Lordship of Mold in the County*
*of Flint and of Llanverras in the County*
*of Denbigh by the High Court of Exchequer*
*at Westminster 10th November 1763.*

Witnesses brought forward at the time of the various lawsuits provided details of the ancient custom of "beating the bounds". Amongst other (sometimes even more robust) practices, "Children who walked the parish boundary with aged inhabitants were made to remember important landmarks by having their ears pinched, by being beaten with twigs and whips, or being thrown into the river."

The dispute led the artist Richard Wilson to paint an inn sign which depicts two heads looking in opposite directions and an inscription which reads: "*We Three Loggerheads*" – inviting the observer to identify himself as the third party. A copy of the painting is displayed inside the pub; it is very dark and benefits from close-up viewing. It shows two bald men, head to (back of) head almost morphed into one Zaphod Beeblebrox-like character. Both have their eyes closed, unable even to look at each other. The character on the left has his nose in the air, a long pipe clutched to his chest. His counterpart on the right has a look of Lenin about him: he has a stiff

*Carreg Carn March Arthur*

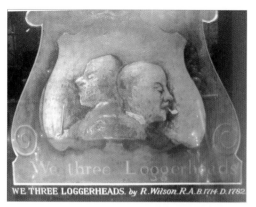

W.E. THREE LOGGERHEADS. *by R.Wilson.R.A.B.1714.D.1782*

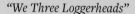

*"We Three Loggerheads"*

*Mining legacy at Loggerheads country park*

starched collar and a curiously short pipe in his mouth. The original is thought to be lost.

Loggerheads is not the only place name in the area to have resulted from mining. A short distance up the hill in the direction of Mold is Cadole. Until the 1950s the village was known as Cathole, owing, it is said, to a cat having being found in a mine shaft there. The original name lives on in the "Cathole lead vein" which lies beneath the village.

We follow the busy riverside path. There are large family groups, doting grandmothers tilt their heads at babies in prams and children run, throwing sticks in the river. There is an educational trail which they can follow to learn of the industrial past and the great outdoors. I have attended a several very good warden-guided walks here.

We see a bench with a memorial plate, look up at the limestone cliff and are reminded of the time we came here on one of our early Sunday morning walks. We had strolled along the quiet pre-visitor riverbank, and then made our way up to the top to enjoy a breakfast sandwich and flask of tea. We sat there, the early sun warming us up. At this juncture a chap entered the scene stage right and proceeded to scatter ashes out of an urn on to the cliff top. A lovely place to be laid to rest and a lovely spot to have breakfast; two activities which shouldn't coincide...

Pentre Mill was used to grind corn from the late eighteenth century. A watercolour in the care of the National Library of Wales by John Ingleby dated 1796, "*View from the Loggerheads*", shows a mill with a wheel fed by a leat in the approximate position of the current building. It was used as a saw-mill from the late nineteenth century and produced electricity until 1942 – a versatile piece of kit. The workings have been renovated; the leats cleaned out and the wheel turns once more.

Old mine workings and buildings are located right next to the river. Water was both the problem and solution in relation to one aspect of the mines. The lead occurs in the limestone base rock which, as we have already seen, is notoriously porous. Shafts over 600ft deep were sunk to access the precious ore, into which water would percolate.

The leat which feeds Pentre Mill was also used to power two waterwheels, on opposite sides of the Alun, which operated

*Pentre Mill (Loggerheads)*

a system of rods to dewater the Glan Alyn mines. The stone pit which housed the wheel on the west bank can still be seen. An information board on the path above the pit reads:

"In front of you are the ruins of a wheelpit that housed a huge 40ft waterwheel, used to pump water from the Glan Alyn mine. The wheelpit was built in the 1860's when the wheel on the opposite

*Grey wagtail on the old waterwheel wall*

*Wild garlic in spring at Loggerheads*

bank was no longer powerful enough to keep the mine dry."

An illustration shows the leat supplying water over the top of the wheel. The shaft is connected to an arrangement of rods which can be seen disappearing into the mine entrance. They are carried on supporting posts which appear to have rollers on the top. One can only imagine the potential problems with this system of so many variables. Mechanical energy – first rotary, then horizontal(ish) had to be transferred by the rods over the river to the opposite bank, and then vertically downward into the shaft (the board mentions it pumped water from 165ft underground). The power for this system would have been supplied by a cantankerous Alun with its highly changeable flow – susceptible to freezing, withering to nothing and flooding. (In 2000, over 100 days of consecutive rainfall caused the Alun to flood at Loggerheads, Rhydymwyn, Mold and Rossett). That such lengths were undertaken to access the ore, further reinforces its high value.

The illustration shows a second leat on the opposite bank feeding a pump house containing the original smaller wheel, a similar set of rods leading toward the mine. The demands on the Alun as a power source here were legion: in this case, fighting water with water.

*Spring at Loggerheads*

# 8. The Leete and Devil's Gorge

Dappled sunlight filters through the trees; the people thin out as the aroma of delicious coffee from the cafe is left behind us. Signs indicate "The Leete path" – I knew I'd seen the name somewhere!

Leats can take many forms, both physically and in spelling. The Great Leete was built to supply the Pen-y-fron mine, by John Taylor, a mining entrepreneur and mineral agent to Earl Grosvenor. It is some 3.2km long by 2m wide and 1.5m deep, a considerable feat of engineering.

The path runs parallel to the empty Leete, forming two adjacent paths in some areas. The curved base fills with leaf fall in the autumn, for those blackbird-like walkers who like to stir things up as they go.

The riverbed here is riddled with "sink" or "swallow" holes which steal the flow in summer. There is Alun aplenty here today.

All manner of methods were tried in efforts to harness the cantankerous Alun. In "The Milwr Tunnel" by Cris Ebbs there is a sketch of the Loggerheads area showing work done in the 1930s on numerous swallow holes. He details swallows which were "excavated to depths of up to 22 feet then filled and sealed", as well as showing dams and a section of river diverted to avoid swallows. He further writes of proposals for canalising the bed, and even diverting the whole river by tunnelling through the hill from Loggerheads towards Mold. Thankfully these were shelved on grounds of costs.

Devil's Gorge (*Ceudwll y Diafol* or *Craig y cythrel*), formed by the mining of calcite (a carbonate mineral common in

*The (empty) Leete and its path*

limestone) in the nineteenth century, is quite spectacular – a chasm cut deep into the cliff, over which a bridge permits the easy conveyance of walkers. At its base an inky black hole leads deep underground. There were no abseilers or climbers on this day, no Technicolor splashes on the sheer grey walls.

The path climbed and the Alun disappeared behind the trees. I was at treetop level but could still hear her frolicking about. Moel Famau came into view: at 554m the highest point in the Clwydian Hills – 1,820ft in old money – dominating all below her. No matter from which angle I chance upon her, she always makes me pause.

The remains of the jubilee tower at the summit make for a fascinating story. Built in the Egyptian style to celebrate the golden jubilee of George III in 1810, it must have been a sight to behold. Crowning Moel Famau with a further 94ft of stone, it would have been visible from afar. However, as is sometimes the manner of these things, the construction was problematic. Fundraising was slow; plans were scaled back and building work was not to the standard of the Pharaohs whom the architect sought to emulate. It was

dealt its final blow by a storm in 1862. In these days of the Angel of the North and other such large-scale public works, who knows, in the future another grand scheme may once again crown the queen of the Clwydian Hills.

The Clwydians are home to numerous hill forts, but Moel Famau, despite being the highest peak and having a convenient plateau at the top, was never fortified;

*The Devils Gorge*

possibly it had too much spiritual significance. Moel Famau translates as Mother's Mountain, an echo of Mother Earth/Pacha Mama. What *would* the Iron Age folk have made of Egyptian-style Georgian bling on their sacred mountain?

There was a steep drop now to the left: this stretch is known as Precipice Walk. Buzzards circled above and a heron lumbered slowly across the valley, the Vulcan bomber of the bird world.

Inscriptions in the low wall helpfully point the way to Loggerheads and advise: "Go slow – narrow path." No one to sue in those days; if you fouled up it was your own fault. *Stercus Accidit.*

From Trial Bridge onward to Rhydymwyn, my map offered a choice of two paths following the Alun Valley from the Cilcain road. I opted for the high-level path continuing along the Leete, rather than the lower riverside track. This is a quiet section of the river: few people venture this far from Loggerheads. The path brought me to an area of raised ground where the path and the Leete diverge. The footpath continued straight ahead up the steep slope, while the Leete bore left along the contour line, hidden by dense undergrowth and holly thickets. After a quick recce of its overgrown state, I decided to follow the path, which I assumed would rejoin the Leete at some stage. Further down the valley a path did, to be sure, coincide with a leat, and although interrupted by many fallen trees,

*Debris at the base of the Loggerheads cliffs*

*Go Slow (wise counsel)*

was passable and led me to an end point close to the Rhydymwyn works site... as I was expecting. At this point I gave myself a pat on the back, having, I thought, followed the 3.2km of the Great Leete from Loggerheads to Rhydymwyn.

A while later, having received correspondence from the Welsh Mills Society concerning mills in this area and armed with the grid reference of Nant Alyn Mill, I arrived at its approximate location – the entrance to the secluded and tranquillo Leete Valley Caravan Park – just as a car pulled up. I seized the opportunity to ask the driver if he knew whether the Nant Alyn mill as detailed by the WMS still existed in any form.

Serendipity smiled on me, as he turned out to be the current occupier of the building stood in front of us, which had indeed once housed the mill and is now the reception building of the park which his family have run for close to 100 years. He showed me the gable end furthest from the river, which dates from around 1650 and would have carried the wheel. This would have been fed by a leat from the west side of the Alun – the opposite side of the river to the Great Leete. Originally a lead ore mill, it was later used for corn.

He went on to explain that the flow from the Great Leete was divided near the raised section I had encountered previously.

As I followed the course of the Leete, I had noticed that for a structure designed to convey water, it no longer seemed to gather the wet stuff. Thoughts had rattled about in my head of how much water would be lost on its long journey owing to leaks, evaporation, etc. Yet here, approximately two thirds of the way to its destination, its flow was divided. There was sufficient remaining flow for the Great Leete to become several leats. A partly quarried out and partly walled channel, much time and effort must have been spent ensuring the expensively re-directed water didn't perform another great escape.

He recommended I consult *The Lead mines of the Alyn Valley* by C.J. Williams, the details of which I eagerly scribbled down.

When I got hold of a copy of the said book, my simplistic view, already dented, that there was one Leete which ran from Loggerheads and fed the foundry at Rhydymwyn, was now well and truly blown out of the water, if you pardon the pun. Three leats are shown on the east bank: "The Leete"; "Middle Leat" and

"Lower Leat" – all of which terminate at the Pen-y-fron (Bryncelyn) mine. (I was much pleased to see the various spellings of leat – even on the same illustration). Two further leats are shown downstream, feeding directly from the Alun and arrowing towards the Rhydymwyn foundry. In my earlier daydream walk, I must have veered off the Great Leete when the going got tough and inadvertently joined the latter leat to the foundry, convincing myself that I had followed the Leete from its beginning to terminus and further that, if I were a boy scout, I could justifiably have claimed my leat-following badge. I must pay more attention from now on.

So with book in hand and mixed feelings of a new adventure and déjà vu I crossed the Mold- Cilcain road once more. This time I continued along the Great Leete to where the path and the Leete diverged, to follow it to its end point without deviating, blinkers on as it were. This was not an easy task. The day gifted to me for this purpose was a very wet one. I sat out the worst of the downpour during the morning and started off in the lighter rain of mid-day. The holly and young saplings soon gave way to full-on dense thickets, almost impassable. I hopped over and under fallen birch trees, strangled by ivy. Thick, thick moss and leaves covered all the fallen debris, making every step hazardous. Near the road at Pen-y-fron Chapel the Leete was obliterated by a wide track which leads down to the old limestone quarry.

On the other side of the track, the trail ran cold. I continued along the contour of the hill, pursuing the same approximate course as the Leete logically should have followed. This area proved to be even more overgrown, with lots more holly and trees, and also with bundles of cut branches and waste which appeared to have been fly-tipped from the road above. I thought I could see a vague channel but it was full of debris, including an old cooker, some corrugated sheeting and an oil drum. I progressed very slowly, wet and tired, over and under fallen trees, eventually picking up the Leete again as the amorphous vegetation and rubbish gave way to natural holly, coppiced hazel and ash. I had never seen so much holly in one place, it was the springy variety, which wasn't fun to bend out of the way; sometimes it committed acts of spiky and painful flagellation in revenge. I crossed another path and thankfully the Leete was again clearly visible; not only this, but I could see another leat running parallel on the slope below me. Things were looking up, and improved further when I arrived at the big Inca-like stone walls of the Pen-y-fron mine. The Great Leete finishes its journey here on the dressing floor, 3.2 km after leaving the Alun at Loggerheads. The middle leat offshoot also ends here lower down the mine workings; it could supply either the dressing floor or the wheel at Waterwheel Shaft as required. A third "lower" leat running directly from the Alun upstream of Cilcain Bridge also fed the wheel at Waterwheel Shaft. The waterwheel here must have been critical to the workings. An earlier wheel here was fed via a launder by an eighteenth century leat from the west bank of the Alun. This crossed the Alun at Nant Alyn Mill, now occupied by the caravan park reception, which it later also supplied. This is shown on a watercolour of 1796 by J. Ingleby which is reproduced on the cover of the book.

Another leat is shown in the book as coming from a wholly unexpected easterly direction to the Pen-y-fron mine. It is labelled as "Leat from Pantymwyn Mine".

Troublesome water pumped out of one mine would be further utilised in downstream workings so nothing was wasted. The pumping of water and flows in leats must have been a complex affair requiring close co-ordination to ensure safe access to the mines in all states of water, and reliable supply to multiple users. I wonder if there was an overall controller of these activities on a daily basis – a bit like the "Aquarius" in Robert Harris' Pompeii.

The Mold Mines were remarkable in the Taylor era for the quantity of water pumped from them. He claimed that "more water was lifted by pumps than at any other mine in Britain... often delivering more than 8,000 gallons per minute."

The two leats supplying the Rhydymwyn foundry were possibly originally built to power corn mills before being utilised for mining purposes. They are now hidden by trees; unseen, truncated, redundant. A large stone built wheel housing can be seen near the south side of the road which skirts the Rhydymwyn works site, the last remaining feature of the final leat in this valley of many leats.

Prior to my dalliance with the Alun, as mentioned earlier, I didn't even know what a leat was. I arrived at Rhydymwyn, enlightened in their existence and acquainted with several of them including the wonderful 3.2kms of the Great Leete. The Iron and Brass foundries, initially established by John Taylor in 1836 to service the mines, continued after his withdrawal from the Mold mines in 1845. They turned to making mining machinery for export, moving to Sandycroft in 1862, where they operated until 1925.

Just before Rhydymwyn, a lane leads off the valley road up the hill to Coed Du Hall. Some years ago, on a nearby walk, I chatted to a local of the parish who told me of a "font" at the roadside somewhere in this area where it is thought baptisms were once performed. Having seen nothing along the valley road, I followed the lane, expecting, from what I had heard, to see some kind of stone sink built into the wall. I came to a roofless building with church-like arched windows next to the lane, – I could see where the baptism theory came from, but a large sunken bath taking up half the room did not stand out as been practical for baptisms – not unless they were full immersion affairs. The word

on the streets is this was a bathing house for the ladies of Coed Du.

Now a romantic ruin, but could it become a restoration project in the future? Who knows? On this day the 'bath' was full, fed by a nearby spring, possibly awaiting the badgers from the sett at its rear to enjoy a frollicky soak under a full moon? I'd like to think so.

Coed Du Hall, built in 1811, is now a hospital. Once home to John Taylor, it is a large and pleasingly located building, sitting in a wooded area, to an open-front aspect. Taylor was evidently a mover and shaker: he owned many of the Mold mines, and rubbed shoulders with the great and the good.

*1. Old stonework near the Waterwheel Shaft;*
*2. Rhydymwyn Bath house*

# 9. WMD

*"A poet can write about a man slaying a dragon, but not about a man pushing a button that releases a bomb."*

W. H. Auden

Arriving at Rhydymwyn village, the ubiquitous mill cottage still exists on the west side of the Alun. The large Rhydymwyn flour mill operated here until 1930 and was demolished in 1966; the site is now occupied by modern housing. A corn mill is recorded in Rhydymwyn as far back as 1587.

A plaque in the village commemorates a visit by Mendelssohn:

"Felix Mendelssohn Bartholdy, born at Hamburg 1809, died 1843 [Sic], composed 'the rivulet' in 1829 while visiting Mr. ---- Taylor, who rented Coed-Du."

Mr. Taylor's Christian name appears to have been corrected: the names John and Henry are superimposed. I wonder if this was a simple old-fashioned cock-up or a Pharaoh-like attempt to re-write history; either way, a slight blemish to the memory of the Leete and mine man. Not wanting to criticise a form of public information which I really enjoy, and without knowing the history of the plaque, the fact that Mendelssohn actually died in 1847 would seem to support the former hypothesis.

Charles Kingsley, clergyman, professor, historian and author of many works including "The Water Babies" and another leat walker, is similarly commemorated.

Lead mining in the Rhydymwyn area goes right back to Roman times. Rhydymwyn translates as "ford of the ore".

The Alun has reached its northernmost point and now does one of its about-turns, heading in a broadly south-east direction on another adventure. On a winter's day I watched its full flow going through the concrete walls of the flood alleviation scheme, built after the flood of 2000 and under the old valley works site (built on the older foundry site). It has also reached its westerly watershed. To the west of Rhydymwyn, water flows into the river Wheeler/afon Chwiler and on into the Clwyd near Bodfari – this is another gentle watershed not altogether obvious from topography.

Although Rhydymwyn today is a quiet country village, it has a fascinating history.

A plaque at the secured entrance (small village, many plaques) reads:

> *"This is the site of the Ministry of Supply valley works, developed in 1939 for the wartime production of mustard gas, its storage in underground chambers and the assembly of chemical munitions. Some of the earliest research in support of the development of the atomic bomb was also undertaken here.*
>
> *Valley works was a facility of great wartime importance, employing over 2,000 people whose contribution to the war effort was considerable.*
>
> *The site is now a haven for wildlife and nature conservation."*

I can verify the last sentence; I've enjoyed several excellent events here. The work done is all the more outstanding given the nature of the nasty stuff produced here in the past. Unfortunately, today it is closed.

Fascinating guided tours are occasionally conducted here. It was the only UK wartime installation not located by German intelligence. Had it been found and bombed, the effect on the village and the surrounding area could have been disastrous. Many of the buildings were pulled down during decommissioning, but a railway siding coated in rubber to prevent sparks is an eerie reminder of the explosive goods produced here. Work was also done here on enriching uranium that involved some scientists who went on to be part of the Manhattan project, the U.S. government research that produced the first atomic bombs.

A leaflet produced for the Rhydymwyn nature reserve gives an absorbing overview of the comprehensive transformation this mile-long site has undergone. A map is identified by two keys: red numerical symbols highlight locations of historical interest; areas of wildlife interest are shown alphabetically in yellow.

*Rubber coated railway platform*

Building Number 45 nearest the visitor centre encapsulates the regeneration of the site: number one in the red key advises that it "used to house gaseous diffusion experiments in support of developing methods for uranium enrichment in the early days of the atomic bomb project". The same spot is marked with a yellow B explaining: "the valley is important for eight bat species. Building 45, for instance, provides conditions required by long-eared and the rare lesser horseshoe bat."

Other areas on the map follow this pattern. The "toxic burial pit" and main tunnel entrance sit adjacent to the bird hide and the wetland area. The tunnel "along with two others, extend more than 200m into the hillside. Connected to these are four storage chambers used to house bulk mustard gas and filled chemical munitions."

Further reclaimed areas show orchids, grass snakes, badger setts and signs of otter use. From WMD to nature reserve: that's a commendable transformation.

*A previous life*

# 10. Magicked Away/Hesb Alun

I have often heard it said that in the summer when the Alun disappears, it does not vanish completely; it reappears downstream, returned to its bed, like a naughty child after an underground sojourn. Logically this resurrection must happen, as the Alun continues to flow further downstream when the Loggerheads area is dry as a funeral drum. I decided to revisit this stretch in July, to try to pinpoint the spot where the Alun emerges triumphant from the underworld.

From the stone bridge at Loggerheads I walked 578 paces along the Alun to where it flowed no further. It gathered in a pool, from the edge of which I could hear the sound of it gurgling away underground, via a sinkhole, into the embrace of Mother Earth.

Downstream at Hope that very morning, the Alun had been in positively rude health, so logically it must at some point have reappeared in its bed. Or is it some kind of Zen riddle: When is a river not a river? Or a high-school geography exam question perhaps: "A river arises at grid reference A6, has no middle section

*Dry Alun*

and flows into another river at grid reference B4. Explain how this happens with aid of sketches."

I continued along the dry bed, under a redundant bridge. I had used this crossing point in the winter and witnessed a boisterous flow here. On this day, however, not a drop of water was to be seen. It felt strange; the riverbed was my path, the ground felt solid below my feet and yet a complete river had disappeared. I wondered if there was a system of caverns below me extending upward to just a few millimetres under my feet, covered by the lightest dusting of gravel, the last delicate ceiling section of some vast cavern, just waiting for the final act of erosion to destroy its millennia of layers of geology and trick me into a sudden journey downwards into a very deep rabbit-hole.

It is very likely no coincidence that Lewis Carroll was raised in Ripon, an area renowned for its sink holes. In Ripon's case the bedrock is gypsum, even more soluble than limestone. The underground cave system there is periodically troublesome, collapsing to swallow up chunks of fields, garages, that sort of thing. Carroll must have been aware of the hungry sink holes, written large in local folklore. They could well have been the inspiration for his "down the rabbit-hole" story.

Ironically rain had started to fall, speckling the limestone chunks over which I picked my way. Occasional patches of gravel offered a less ankle-twisting route.

I saw the entrance to some old mine workings on the right at the base of the cliff. It was Bible black in there so I didn't enter, but someone obviously had, for at its mouth there were containers, presumably for the removal of ore: one a simple bucket, the other a trough-like container, with a rough length of rope still attached for dragging it along. Nearby on the ground lay a hammer with a large chunky head. I reached down to pick it up. It was much heavier than it looked; I wouldn't have wanted to wield it for a full shift, but it must have been a valued possession for a miner. I wondered what circumstances had led to its being left behind; possibly a hasty exit from a dangerous situation, or simply mislaid? A thought entered my head saying it would

make a good exhibit at the Loggerheads shop. Another, more sensible thought popped up in the practical part of my brain, whichever side that is, which pointed out I was heading *away* from the shop and further I'm no Geoff Capes. So after this debate with myself I walked on, hammerless, slipping and sliding on the rain-wet rocks.

Walking along a dry river bed in the rain reminded me of the time I went to Death Valley. On the way there, the guide had spoken at great length quoting lots of statistics as to its incredible dryness. I alighted at Furnace Creek for the afternoon; it rained, twice.

Dry, dry, dry.

As I weaved my way along I came across occasional isolated pools of stagnant water. A couple of hundred yards shy of Trial Bridge I saw a flow of water up ahead. It must be true; the Alun does re-emerge! But on closer inspection my hopes were dashed. A culvert flowed from the left, having emanated from beneath the hills which stretch up to Moel Famau. Clear, fresh water spilled out, covering about a third of the river bed. My shadow on the water caused fish to dart about, but offered little cover for the poor blighters.

The demi-Alun trickled for a short distance only, under the bridge into some murky pools where it was halted by a ridge of gravel. Trial Bridge is so called because of the steep approaches to the Alun valley of the Mold – Cilcain road where motorcycle trials were once held.

This area on the map is aptly labelled Hesb Alun. *Hesb* translates as dry or barren. For those with troglodyte tendencies there are entrances to large cave systems in this area. The narrow horizontal entrance to Poachers' Cave is in the cliff, next to the lower of the two paths along this stretch. I assumed its name derived from its use as a hiding place, but then learnt that its Welsh name was totally different – Ogof Hen Ffynhonnau – *the cave of the old wells*. Was the English name down to some difficulty in pronunciation? Not at all; cavers are a competitive lot! There is considerable kudos to be gained from being the first to explore a system fully or find an unexplored system. The access to this cave was being dug by one club, but another group then broke through, allegedly "poaching it".

*1. Dry Alun valley in Spring; 2. Small streams attempt to replenish the dry Alun valley*

Another cave in this area is called Ogof Nadolig or *Christmas Cave*, after the day it was found. They must have been a pretty keen lot, these cavers, forgoing turkey and James Bond for their sport. Further on is the portal to Ogof Hesb Alun, which is well known in the caving community; it's right next to the river bank and goes vertically downward into the bowels of the earth. I'm sure there are fantastic things to see down there, but I am more than happy to leave them to cavers and dwarves.

Further downstream hazy sunshine filtered through the leaves and reflected off water. Aha! As I got closer, I could see pools of water populated by tadpoles. My hopes were once more raised but the flow didn't spring forth from the river bed after a mysterious underground rollercoaster journey; it emanated from a sewage treatment works. Not only that, it fizzled out after a couple of hundred yards.

A large abandoned quarry opened up on the right of the river; the hillside cut back, leaving sheer limestone cliffs. Over a footbridge, on the western side of the river, almost hidden by ivy and fallen trees, lay the remains of a lead mill.

The river bed from here on was increasingly colonised by plant life, nettles, and sycamore saplings and, the furthest upstream I have noticed it, Himalayan Balsam. To dampen my spirits further; the single rain cloud allocated to North Wales for that morning by the BBC reappeared, and having gained in strength on its circuitous route, proceeded to drench me.

There was positively no flow at Rhydymwyn; the "Danger – Deep Water" signs at the entrance to the valley site looked idly on. I can therefore conclude that on that particular July day the healthy flow of the Alun fizzled out downstream from the stone bridge at Loggerheads and did not reappear in its bed. In other years with greater rainfall the flow may re-emerge, but on that day it was spirited away from the water course known as the Alun.

There is much evidence to support the re-emergence or, if you will, resurrection of the Alun – a copy of a map on the wall at Mold Museum titled: "Mold hundred from William Williams' new map of the counties of Denbighshire and Flintshire c.1720" is marked with an 'a' just north of Colomendy, roughly at the same point I saw the Alun gurgle away, and with a 'b' some distance downstream toward Rhydymwyn. The letters are joined by a dotted line following the course of the Alun and have the following note: "The river runs underground from a to b being almost two miles".

Thomas Pennant in his tour of north Wales in 1773 writes of the Alun sinking under the ground "like the sullen mole and continues a subterraneous course for half a mile before emerging to the day".

Cris Ebbs further mentions that, prior to mining, Ogof Hesb Alun was flooded, taking its water from the swallow holes and returning it to the river bed at a spring east of Cilcain near Hesb Alun. "Ystrad Alun" recounts a trial carried out in the 1970s, whereby dye put in the swallow holes at Glan Alun, was seen to emerge at Hesb Alun, some 2.6km and 24 hours later.

The neo-Alun was, to my eyes, fed by springs further down from under the valley works. I continued downstream and viewed a larger flow under the Mold-Denbigh road. Further tributaries joined to give the merry flow I viewed on my evening walk at Hope.

The Alun has always been robbed of its flow by the thirsty bedrock to some extent, but mining activity has broken through underground caverns in the limestone, increasing the water loss.

Water seepage into the lead workings, as already seen, had been a real problem. As well as surface attempts to make the Alun watertight, underground efforts were made to drain the water away. The most notable of these draining tunnels was the Milwr Tunnel.

Ten miles in length, it extended from the Loggerheads area, passing close to the village of Milwr, and on to the coast near Bagillt. Started in 1897, it was an extraordinary feat of engineering. Its very existence is testament to the value of the precious lead ore locked deep underground. It allowed over 50 veins to be worked right down to sea level, creating over 60 miles of interconnected passageways in the process.

The de-watering, however, had a serious unintended consequence. On the 5th of January, 1917 workers in the tunnel broke into a flooded passage, releasing a huge outflow of water. Several hours later, the renowned St Winefride's well, several miles away in Holywell dried up.

In the seventh century, Winefride (*Gwenfrewi*) resisted the advances of a local prince, who in his anger decapitated her. Where the severed head fell, a miraculous healing well sprung forth. Winefride was restored to life by her uncle, St Beuno (protector of curlews).

The Holy Well, a site of devout pilgrimage for a millennium and a half, was deprived of its healing waters. Not only this, but the people of Holywell lost their water supply and the industrial mills in the Greenfield valley were without their power source.

The water flow seen at the well today was diverted (after a drought of some 37 weeks) from another area of old mine workings to the north-west of Holywell.

St Winefride's Well for believer or non-believer has an incredible history: from its miraculous beginnings, to its very survival in the severe penal period to the present day as a continuing Catholic shrine; the well is a place of calm and serenity. A dip in its icy waters, which flow at a constant 5 degrees centigrade, is, I can personally attest, bracing and highly recommended. "St Winefride, Her Holy Well and the

*St Winefride's Well, Holywell*

Jesuit Mission, C.650-1930" by T.W. Pritchard is a wonderfully enlightening account of the history of the well.

The Milwr Tunnel, although the most well known, is not the only drainage tunnel; there are others and together they drain millions of gallons of water daily.

It could be argued that the Alun, particularly in the summer months, is actually two completely separate rivers: the "original" Alun rises above Llandegla and flows to the Loggerheads – Rhydymwyn area, from where it is whisked away via sink holes and drainage tunnels, under Halkyn Mountain, and on into the Dee estuary; the "neo" Alun has its source in the springs between Rhydymwyn and Mold and flows onwards to the river Dee downstream of Holt and Farndon. It could further be argued that the man-made shortcut turns the clock back millions of years, returning the Alun to its pre-Ice Age northerly course.

I wonder what the total effect of all the losses is on the volume of water in the lower Alun. It has undoubtedly been robbed of its flow since the beginnings of time, but standing at the outfall of the Milwr Tunnel and seeing its re-directed flow into the Dee estuary, it is clear that the pre-Industrial Revolution flow of the Alun was much greater than it is today. The Milwr Tunnel discharges an average flow of 23 million gallons per day into the Dee, rising to 36 million gallons in wet weather. Two thirds of this water is from two cave systems intersected by the workings.

The last lead mine in the area, Olwyn Goch at nearby Hendre, closed in 1986, bringing nearly 2000 years of production to an end.

*Milwr tunnel outflow – the waters of the Alun reunited*

# 11. A New Beginning – Alleluia!

I joined the neo-Alun at the downstream side of the Rhydymwyn works on a cold winter's day when the Alun was in full flow. The ground underfoot was solid, the landscape opened up, the tree shrouded tunnel-like paths of Loggerheads lay behind me, and the Alun was reborn into the light.

The Loggerheads to Rhydymwyn stretch today is safe, a place to frolic and relax, a delight. In earlier times of industrial hard graft, of scratching a living from cold lonely wet chasms in the ground, I'm guessing one's emergence into the open spaces would have been very welcome relief.

For reasons known only to the psychiatric profession, on this day's walk I opted to wear my leather boots which are no longer waterproof, jeans and baseball cap. I left my wellingtons, over-trousers and thick bobble hat in the car.

The path down to the river was steep, covered in wet leaves, and very slippery. A low co-efficient of friction between boot and Mother Earth conspired with gravity to speed me downhill in an uncontrolled fashion. Outstretched arms grasping at the swiftly passing branches provided some, but far from complete, braking effect to slow my ascent. I ended my routine with a ten-foot freestyle backward slide before, thankfully, arriving at the steel fencing at the bottom of the hill still vertical. A fall here would have been very messy.

I heard, and then saw, the Alun breaking free from its confines. It is culverted underground for most of the Rhydymwyn site. The flow in the channel was straight and smooth, orderly, laminar. It surged over a weir and crashed to freedom, white water tumbling around rocks, over fallen tree trunks, at liberty to take its own path along the valley floor. I crossed a footbridge, the brilliant blue of a kingfisher (*glas y dorlan*) streaking with great purpose across the gloom.

The meandering Alun crashed into and undermined its own banks. I saw a recently collapsed section, water swirling around the base of the newly exposed old

1. *'Leaves on the line'*; 2. *St Garmon*

railway embankment where wooden boards had been placed to limit her wandering. The path of the old Mold to Denbigh railway line used to share the valley floor with the Alun until Dr Beeching made it a widow. A little further on a section of the line still exists, albeit now overgrown. There is even some old rolling stock and points, quietly rusting away.

The river snaked and curved, old banks thirty feet away betrayed an earlier course and the soft earth had fresh burrows: home to a fox or badger. Tracks on my side of the river indicated fox cub. Large stones on the banks guided the river on its way.

I saw lots of tennis balls held up at snag points, if there's a club upstream, they may not be troubling Wimbledon for a while yet. This section was cold and wild, I didn't see another soul.

On a nearby hill stands the grade II listed Alleluia Monument erected in 1736 to commemorate St Germanus (our old friend St Garmon) and the Christian Welsh victory over the heathen Picts and Saxons, who were carrying desolation

through the country. Legend has it that St Garmon baptised the Welsh in the Alun before the battle and counselled them to chant "Alleluia!" in unison which was amplified by the surrounding hills, "striking terror into the enemy who fled on all sides; numbers perished by the sword and numbers in the adjacent river".

The Alun in this area is now channelled and pretty shallow, clearly incapable of troubling an army. Back in 429, however, it would have been unfettered; the flood plain would have been a much wilder place as mining had yet to deal its subterranean blow to the volume of river. In a time of flood, on a misty day in a state of panic, who knows, the Alun may indeed have played a significant part in the battle.

The monument stands on the brow of a hill next to a strip of trees, clearly visible from the road. Strange, then that it took me two attempts to find it. In the dusty memories of my mind I came here in the 1980s and it was located on an open, sloped area. Either it has been moved or, more likely, the old memory has been ravaged by time and events.

The solid base of the monument certainly didn't look like it had qualified for any air miles; not even air yards. The soft sandstone of the torso was not as resilient; a weather-beaten Latin inscription on the north face was barely legible.

I walked back to the road, wondering if I were to return again in another 30 years, God willing, whether the monument will have moved again, across this landscape which can, after all, swallow an army.

Close by the monument is Rhual Hall,

*Garmon's Alleluia victory monument*

a country house set within a fine landscaped park. A house is mentioned as being on the site in the 1520s. The present building dates back to 1634. It is Grade 2 listed, having a rare unaltered seventeenth century forecourt layout and bowling green. My map showed no footpaths from which the grounds could be viewed, so I had to content myself with brief glimpses from the road.

On the opposite side of the Alun valley, in country house symmetry, stands Gwysaney Hall, one of the grandest sporting and agricultural estates in North Wales. Gwysaney itself dates back to the ninth century when it was linked with Rhodri Mawr, King of Wales. A programme on S4C showed some of the glorious wood-panelled interior, its grand staircase and dark wood crafted fireplace. A portrait of every person to have lived there was hung on the walls. The original studded front door bears the date 1640; some of its many repairs are said have stemmed from cannon damage sustained when Cromwell's Roundhead forces laid siege to the Royalist house in 1645.

My interest having been whetted by the TV programme, I checked my map and noted that the Gwysaney estate was pleasingly intersected by public footpaths. From the lodge on the Mold–Denbigh road, I followed a half-mile-long drive winding up through trees to the hall at the top of the hill. The warm stone frontage of the hall is very impressive as it sits behind the formal lawn.

The footpath ran in a circular route behind the hall, from where there are spectacular views over the Cheshire plain to Beeston Castle and the Peckforton Hills. Further on, the setting of Gwysaney and its ability to resist the siege could be better appreciated. It sits high atop a steep east-facing hill. The light brown stone gives it a welcoming feel in warm sunlight, but back in war-torn days it must have been a formidable sight. Originally built to an "H" plan, the building at that time had an additional "leg" – the east wing. This was demolished around 1823, when it was found to be in danger of falling down the hill. On the plus side there is now a fantastic bay window in the drawing room. The house was extended westwards to compensate for the loss, resulting in the non-symmetrical, but nevertheless still very impressive, building that survives today.

Right, I'd better get back to the river...

Crossing the Mold – Denbigh road, I came to a yard where trucks were being worked on. The cheery owner asked if I was lost, or if I was from the Environment Agency; he obviously hadn't noticed my flower power wellies. I apologised for veering off the path. "No problem" he said. I told him I was following the Alun. He kindly shared his ample local knowledge, relating how the embankments further downstream used to be higher to prevent flooding and there being many more trees now which can cause blockages and hence inundation. He went on: "We can't clear out the river now...*freshwater shrimps*, we can't cut trees down... *bats*." I said I remembered some flooding in Mold in the early 1980s; he pointed to the defences put in place at the end of his yard after the 2000 floods. The point where we were stood had been six feet under water. He said he didn't think he would see that again in his lifetime; his Gran hadn't seen anything as bad in her years. But if it were to happen, the new defences would be of little help; the water had actually come in from behind the yard, whence it overflowed on to the road.

I later learned that there was major flooding in this area in August 1879. The railway bridge had its supporting masonry washed away by the raging torrent, leaving the rails suspended in mid-air.

Downstream, I rejoined the path which led me into a corn field. A curl of embankment to my left protected a sub-station from the no-no waters of the Alun. I saw the storage tanks and heard the thrum of the chemical plant on the opposite bank. I seem to remember formaldehyde been made here. An impossible image entered my head of a preserved shark. Concrete bunds protected the river, the riparian population living close by in soft earth riddled with holes. An outfall of water drops through a shaft of sunlight onto mossy rocks in a sheltered area of trees, take away the carrier pipe and the industrial background noise and it could be the setting for a shampoo advert.

One lonely worker operated a fork-lift truck. I wondered how long this plant could resist the export of industry to the East. This site has long been used for manufacture. A display in Mold Museum details a grand cotton mill being built here in 1792 by Samuel and James Knight of Manchester. A report in the Manchester Mercury is quoted: "A handsome and stupendous factory"..."in full work and having a competent number of excellent hands...in complete repair....fully equipped with water and the machinery is in excellent condition upon the most improved principles."

Two copies of paintings by J. Ingleby from 1796 confirm the mill's undoubted grandeur. They show a tall, solid building with six rows of windows. The surrounding hills are exaggerated in height in romanticised fashion, and the mill itself may also be subject to artistic licence, but the facts speak for themselves; when it burnt down in 1866 it had 25,000 spindles and employed 250 people.

It wasn't rebuilt owing to the depressed state of the cotton market at that time. The site lay in ruins until it started a new lease of life as the Alyn Tinplate Works in 1874. The chemical plant has been here since 1947.

I came to a set of submerged stepping stones at a river crossing, I gingerly crossed, the force of water pushing each step downstream and the water lapping at the tops of my wellies, but I traversed safely and felt pretty smug at having (unusually) made the correct choice of footwear.

The river meandered powerfully, crashing from bank to bank. If this were New Zealand I'm sure adventurous types would be whooping and cheering as they careered downstream on some form of floating fun.

The river straightened and quietened. I paused to look at a blown-over willow tree; its base exposed showing its roots like a can-can dancer flashing her thighs. The tree lives on; branches head skywards in search of sunlight from the now horizontal trunk.

This area is popular with dog walkers who can stroll down from the town to administer canine aqua therapy. On a summer walk here I enjoyed watching goldfinches bathing at the water's edge before heading up into the trees to shake themselves dry. As I left them to their natural spa self-pampering I noticed a kestrel on the telephone wires which parallel the river. It swooped down into the long grass, emerging a minute or so later with a small mammal. It flew back up onto the wires holding its prey in its claws and tearing off pieces to slowly digest, coughing up occasional pellets of fur or bone onto the ground below. An impressive act of balancing helped to fill the stomach of this thinking kestrel. No energy-sapping hovering for him. I chatted to a man here who had seen a white bird of prey on the same wires; he described it to an ornithologist friend who thought it could have been a migrating osprey.

I turned my head, looked over to Mold and pictured the Alun, just over the hill at Loggerheads, from where it proceeded to semi-circle Mold. If the scheme proposed to alleviate flooding of the lead mines at Loggerheads by diverting the Alun via a tunnel had gone ahead, it would possibly have re-emerged in this area. This would have taken a couple of miles off its length but, paradoxically, would have increased the flow in its lower reaches.

St Mary's church as seen from this lower perspective is even more imposing, uncluttered by the high street. I can imagine folks down here on bygone summer evenings, laughing and frolicking as they wash their smalls in the river, the church always casting a watchful eye over them.

# 12. Yr Wyddgrug – land of our fathers

*"Nid i'r doeth a'r deallus yr ysgrifennais, ond i'r dyn cyffredin"* – "Not for the wise and learned have I written, but for the common people."

*Daniel Owen*

Mold is the largest settlement on the Alun, a busy market town retaining many independent businesses and home to the fine Clwyd Theatr Cymru.

The most famous son of Mold is Daniel Owen, preacher, first chairman of Mold urban district council and generally regarded as the father of the Welsh language novel. Whenever an author comes to my attention, I am always curious about their personal lives. What were their influences, what compelled them to write?

Daniel Owen was born in the town in 1836, youngest of six children. The following year his father and two of his brothers were among 21 miners killed in a flooding disaster at Argoed Colliery. A collection made after the disaster was deposited in a bank, which promptly went bust.

Daniel was apprenticed to a tailor, who, along with his church minister, noticed his potential and encouraged him to write. His works give a vivid account of Welsh life in Victorian times and the huge influence of

*The novelist's statue in Mold*

the church. A large section of Mold Museum (above the library) is given over to him.

His fireside tales *Straeon y Pentan* is a collection of short stories of simple everyday life, sometimes told in the style of a parable. They give a window into that epoch and the preceding era. Although life was undoubtedly tough, he saw the church and improved education as having bettered the lot of the common man; superstition and belief in the supernatural is largely displaced by knowledge and faith, although ghosts still play a prominent part in some of his stories. For me they bring back childhood memories of sitting by the fireside with Nain and Taid, friends and family calling in for no particular reason other than to chat, exchange stories and 'pass time.' The site of his tailor's shop is now a public house, its name being an abbreviation of the title. A plaque on the wall commemorates him.

The colliery disaster which took away Daniel Owen's father and brothers is a reminder of the coal-mining history of the Mold area. Of the numerous collieries, the last to survive was Bromfield which closed during the First World War. Their importance is vividly illustrated by the Mold riots of 1869. Unrest, particularly at nearby Leeswood was sparked by poor working conditions, reduced rates of pay and the engaging of workers from outside the area. This culminated in rioting which left four people dead, shot by soldiers brought in from Chester to restore order.

At Bailey Hill an information board has a timeline chronicling the building of the castle in C1100, how it changed hands five times between English and Welsh control between 1146 and 1276. It further records Mold being taken by Parliamentarians, and then re-captured by Royalists in 1644, before Cromwell's forces took Mold again in 1648. In a downpour, at Sunday lunchtime, a winding path took me through oak, chestnut, beech, red-berried holly and yew trees to the top of the fortification. In Norman times it must have looked formidable from the flood plain of the Alun below.

St Mary the Virgin church is set back off the high street, which continues rising upwards to Bailey Hill, which pips her in

*1. 12th century church masonry in garden wall near Bailey Hill; 2. The old bowling green; 3. The Gorsedd stone circle at Bailey Hill, used for the proclamation of the National Eisteddfod of 1923*

the altitude stakes. A blue plaque, kindly placed by Mold civic society, reads:

*Saint Mary's Parish Church c.1490.*
*Built by Margaret Beaufort, mother*
*Of Henry Tudor, to mark his victory*
*at the*
*Battle of Bosworth 1485, which*
*brought the*
*Tudors to the throne.*

Inside it is light and spacious; there are conversations taking place among the pews, a living church. Quiet areas in the chapels at the eastern end offer space for solitude, reflection and prayer.

I pause at a match-stick model of the church and admire the patience which must have gone into its making. A lady seated nearby says it is very popular with the youngsters. She hands me a leaflet which gives a step-by-step guided tour, and points out a few of the features – the thick west wall of the original pre-Stanley church, the window above the vestry door which contains some of the original glass. The end sections are of solid construction, as it was thought the glass would not support the weight above it. "Enjoy," she says as she goes back to her paperwork.

The leaflet gives an overview of thirteenth-century Mold, when two buildings dominated the town: the castle of the Norman barons at Bailey Hill, "Montalt" or "Monte Alto," from which 'Mold' is thought to have derived its name, and the church on this site, first mentioned in 1253.

This building arose at a decisive watershed in Welsh and British history. Margaret Beaufort was the second wife of Lord Stanley, of the manor of Mold, possessor of large estates in North West England, the north-east of Wales and a very big cheese. He was the last to use the title 'King of Mann.' Together they undertook the rebuilding of the "Stanley Churches" at Mold, Gresford and Hope. It was Lord Stanley who placed the crown of Richard III (recently re-buried at Leicester Cathedral) on the head of his own stepson Henry, after the Battle of Bosworth. Richard III was the last English king to die in battle; his death marked the end of the Middle Ages.

It is impossible to mention Margaret Beaufort without giving a very brief overview of this remarkable woman. She gave birth to Henry Tudor at the age of 13 having already become a widow; her

*St Mary the Virgin church Mold*

husband Edmund Tudor (of Penymynydd Anglesey lineage) had died from plague two months earlier. In a time when women had little power, she managed to not only survive the entire wars of the roses, one of the most turbulent and bloodiest periods in our history when a wrong allegiance could result in death, she engineered, schmoozed, manipulated and politicked her way through six regime changes to see her son become king, in the process founding a new dynasty. Not a bad outcome for a young single mum.

St Mary's has a fine oak-panelled roof and carved pews; no two pew ends are the same, there are intricate elephants, unicorns, bears and boars. At the altar, the warden lights candles in preparation for an afternoon wedding. She bemoans the quality of modern church candles.

Old photos of Mold show a row of houses in front of the church. The modern approach is uncluttered but less quirky. Behind the church lies the grave of Richard Wilson. On a local scale he was famous for his Loggerheads Inn sign. He was known far beyond this area: in addition to the brass plaque inside the church, Mold Civic Society has sympathetically commemorated his grave as follows:

*The Tomb of Richard Wilson, 1713–1782*

*"A portrait and landscape artist and one of the founders of the Royal Academy; regarded by many as the father of British landscape painting. Born at Penegoes, near Machynlleth, he was related to the Wynne family of Leeswood Hall and spent much of his childhood in this area. He studied in London under Thomas Wright and later spent time in Venice and Rome, where he gained a reputation as a landscape artist. He returned to London and travelled widely through England and Wales, painting many familiar scenes. He became librarian at the RA before ill health and reduced circumstances forced him to return to live with a cousin at Colomendy Hall, near Mold."*

The Walker Art Gallery in Liverpool contains several Wilson paintings, including "Snowden from Llyn Nantlle – one of the masterpieces of an artist often regarded as the founder of the English landscape school."

To the left of Snowden hangs another Wilson painting, "The valley of the Mawddach" from 1774. Although a similar landscape, this time with Cader Idris as the centre point, it doesn't grab the attention in the same way as Snowden. It's a much flatter, darker work. Even the three people on horseback in the foreground seem to have their heads bowed in tiredness. The detail of the trees is missing, the sky seems empty.

The notes beneath it encapsulate Wilson's demise. "This is a less grand work than Snowden...one of Wilson's last great works. When he painted it, he was beginning to suffer from the alcoholism which ended his career in obscurity and poverty."

Wilson had fallen out with his wealthy patrons. The inn sign was, by some accounts, given in lieu of money owed to the landlord (he had painted at least two other such signs), although Wilson himself disputed this. Tradition has it that he collapsed and died after a stroll along the Alun at Loggerheads surrounded by the scenery he loved so much.

I walked past the town centre livestock market, wonderfully inefficient in its location, it's great to hear the lowing of cattle in a town centre, no disconnect here. An occasional escaped beast causes a frisson of excitement. A path along the old railway line led me back to the Alun; I pondered how transportation and industry moved from rivers and canals to rail, and now to roads; where next on these crowded isles of ours? The bridge over the Mold-Flint road is double-arched and quite grand when viewed from the river, a wooden platform runs under one of the arches, ramped at both ends and raised above the water flow – a secret pan-Alun wildlife highway.

My map shows "Leadmill" in this area, a display at Mold Museum titled "Moldesdale" illustrates an article by Thomas Pennant dated 1778 and quotes "A survey of the mannor of Mold" in 1652. It mentions two mills – a water mill "ye vellyn berved (the middle mill) and a water corn mill in Broncoed "ye vellyn veihan" (the little mill).

I noticed the new houses on the bank here had decking and recreational areas to sit in and appreciate the Alun; older ones had slightly ramshackle sheds and clutter blanking out the river; I wondered if this has been a change of attitude: water courses are now, for the most part, welcomed as havens for wildlife, rather than a resource to be exploited for industry and waste disposal. I came to the hinterland of the rugby and cricket clubs, both of which I occasionally frequented in days of yore on a strictly social basis, my sporting skills having value only in comedy terms. Thereafter, a non-descript field falls gently down to the Alun. On a wall on the opposite side of the row of houses at its far end is a plaque which recalls a find of huge significance at this spot...

*Depiction of the Mold Riots at Grosvenor Hall*

# 13. Tomb Raiders

*"A box without hinges, key, or lid, yet golden treasure inside is hid"*

J. R. R. Tolkien

Now seat ye down, ye good people, lock ye the door, take ye the phone off the hook and make ye comfortable, for what I am about to relate is a fantastic tale indeed...

This area on the southern bank of the Alun is now partially built up, engulfed by urban expansion, but back in 1833 it would have stood undeveloped between a much smaller Mold and the hamlet of Pentre. Known as Bryn-yr-Ellyllon, which translates as *"hill of fiends/ghosts/goblins/elves/sprites"*, it had long been associated with legend and ghostly sightings. The stories generally involved apparitions, glittering in the moonlight; they were reported often enough for the area to be avoided after dark. One such story is said to have been recorded by a local rector from a spooked woman just a few years before.

It must therefore have been an uneasy gang of workmen who approached the barrow to quarry stone. C. H. Leslie in his *Rambles round Mold* (1869), wrote "employment had to be found for able-bodied paupers by the overseers of the parish," and there was in the field what the tenant termed "a big lump of ground." They uncovered a cist containing hundreds of amber beads, several bronze fragments, and the poorly preserved remains of a human skeleton around which was wrapped a thin crushed metal sheet.

The find aroused the curiosity of a local vicar, the Reverend Charles Butler Clough, who wrote:

"Having no idea of the value of their discovery Mr. Langford threw it into a hedge, and told the workmen to bring it with them when they returned home to dinner. In the meantime several persons broke small pieces off it ... rings and breast

*Plaque on Chester Road*

pins have been made out of pieces carried away".

Leslie wrote of these actions: "Alas! That so many Goths were among the crowd...mutilating what would otherwise have been the most valuable antiquity of the kind, any nation could boast of possessing. It proved to be a complete breastplate or gorget, in one entire piece, or sheet of pure beaten gold, beautifully embossed with various patterns, in high relief, over its whole surface – the skeleton within it, as he may have worn it in life, shewing the body had been buried as he fell in battle. The warrior must have been of gigantic proportions, for the part saved measured forty-one inches in length"

The Reverends account came to the attention of the Society of Antiquaries, in far away London. At that time burials from the distant past enjoyed little legal protection. The isolated location of the burial site meant the find could well have been lost forever.

Three years after the spoils from the burial had been divided the British Museum bought from the farmer the first and the largest of the fragments of gold, which had been his share of the booty. Much that the reverend recorded had by that stage disappeared, including virtually the whole skeleton. This left only three large and twelve small crushed and flattened fragments of the decorated gold object.

There being no similar finds in existence to compare it to, it was at one time thought to be a horse peytrel or breastplate, as the nearby plaque erected in 1923 records.

It is easy to see how folklore would lead to this conclusion; a quote from a Miss Angharad Llwyd from 1835 recorded in Mold museum reads:

"The field known as Cae Ellyllon, from stories handed down from one generation

*The Mold Cape at Wrexham Museum*

to another, caused by the appearance of a man of gigantic size, having been seen on several occasions, standing on a tumulus, in the said field...many a tale has been told...of the fright occasioned by the appearance of this formidable spectre".

The name of Benlli Gawr (Benlli the giant) is well recorded in Welsh folklore, such as the stanzas of the graves (*Englynion y Beddau*). His name is further preserved in the local landscape; "Moel Fenlli," Famau's bedfellow, is where he is said to have had his fortress.

It was not until the 1960s that the gold pieces were put together for the first time by the conservators at the British Museum. The flattened fragments of paper-thin gold, with cracks, splits and holes all over them, altogether weighing about half a kilo. It was like a huge three-dimensional jigsaw puzzle, and solving it took nothing less than the re-learning of ancient gold-working techniques that had been lost for millennia. They realised that the curves of the sheet and the flowing lines of the design imitated bead-strings draped over the shoulders. Its size indicates it was made to fit a young boy or woman. The pieces were reassembled into a stunning, punched-gold cape which would have been put over the head, coming down to about the middle of the chest; this would have allowed little movement, pointing toward ceremonial usage.

Formed out of one sheet of the thinnest gold worked from the inside and punched out, this is an object of enormous complexity and ultimate luxury. Crafted in a time when people lived in simple thatched roundhouses, we can only guess whom it was made for.

By studying the precious objects from the grave, gold, amber and bronze, a web of trade and exchange can be tracked that reaches from North Wales to Scandinavia and even to the Mediterranean.

The beautifully reconstructed cape is on display at the British Museum, and was featured in the Radio 4 series 'A history of the world in 100 objects' as object number 19. To give its inclusion some context, its neighbour in the series is a statue to Ramesses II, Ozymandias himself no less, king of kings, who wouldn't reign for another half a millennium.

The Cape is believed to have been made during the early Bronze Age (1900 – 1600 B.C.) and is unique; there really is nothing like it in the whole of Europe. A replica is on display at Mold Museum, labelled as the largest piece of prehistoric gold work found in Britain.

When the burial took place it is likely that the hill overlooked an unconfined Alun. It would have being very visible to approaching upstream and downstream travellers. That the treasures within were not plundered by grave robbers in Valley of the Kings fashion may give an indication of the respect for the deceased person. There is nothing left to see of the "golden barrow" which was 28m in diameter. I wonder if, late on a moonlit night, the occupants of the nearby houses ever catch the faintest glimpse of a shimmering apparition wandering about, 37 centuries after being laid to rest at this spot.

In August 2013, the Mold Cape returned to north-east Wales for a much-welcomed 5-week period in residence at Wrexham County Borough Museum. The Cape was displayed in an illuminated glass case, at the centre of a darkened room, allowing viewing from all angles – I found myself hypnotically circling the case following the flow of the bead indentations: round, oval and square, some with secondary tiny punch marks, as they rose and fell. Having the luxury of the original being on display close by, I viewed it several times, noticing new details on each visit. Some indents are still crushed, and I imagined the cape lying under a mound of rocks, undisturbed for centuries, save for the silent forces of decay and gravity. The joining together of the separate pieces is just visible, slight variations in colour highlight the replaced missing sections, telling a story of a painstaking reconstruction and bringing the Cape to life.

An unexpected bonus from the exhibition was the representation of the discovery of the Mold Cape within a wider context, showing the unusual concentration of Neolithic and early Bronze Age monuments along the Alun valley.

At Llong, one and a half miles south of Mold on the Alun, a large burial monument was excavated. A jet necklace was found scattered amongst the stones of a cairn, which lay over a tightly crouched female skeleton. The necklace was on display along with photographs from the excavations.

Another very large burial monument at Pentrehobin, again just south of Mold, was explored in 2010. This had a deep circular ditch which was 44m in diameter.

The display at Wrexham made reference to fragments of a second gold cape found in the grave and further, there was an extract from a letter suggesting another gold cape may have been discovered nearby:

"A piece of antiquity found not far from Wrexham about two years since; 'twas of Gold, like an Officer's Corselett," (Letter from Richard Mostyn to antiquary Edward Lhuyd, dated 28 February 1694). A comment in the visitor's book at the display mentioned that the old Welsh name for Wrexham was 'Cae'r Fantell', *the field of the cape*, which may support this reference. Yr Wyddgrug may derive from "*gwydd*" tomb and "*crug*" cairn, which may or may not be connected to the Mold Cape site which is a little distance from the historic Mold settlement.

It could be that other capes have existed and since been lost, or indeed are yet to be found, but for the moment the Mold Cape stands unique.

# 14. The Middle Alun

As I left Mold, I became aware that there was more litter about, empty beer bottles and cans. There were tree-houses and rope swings, also lots of young willow trees, some of which had been fenced off to protect them from hungry animals and rampant teenagers. At a delicious bend in the river I disturbed a heron which flew downstream.

A large old building to my right, about 50 feet distant from the river, had a mill-like look about it. As I walked towards it I unintentionally disturbed the heron again; this time, having deduced my direction of travel, it flew upstream. I peered into a ditch in front of the building, at the bottom of which sat two millstones, confirming this as the former Pentre corn mill, now a private dwelling.

Downstream a bridge, invisible from the road, crossed the Alun, a stranded remnant of the old railway line. A turgid grey culvert entered from the nearby industrial estate. Further on, the river had some pleasing deviations. A grove of willow trees formed an amphitheatre capturing the weak winter sun. Fallen branches in places acted as filters, trapping the usual natural debris, as well as bottles, a gas cylinder and what looked like a deflated bouncy castle. Isn't life strange? Soon I arrived at the hamlet of Llong. The Welsh translation of Llong, which is located at the edge of the flood plain, is, not surprisingly, a marsh or swamp. An inn here (1775–1875) was named The Ship, for which the Welsh word is also *Llong*. There's probably a story in this linguistic coincidence which would nicely accompany a pint of stout. The pub had an appropriate inn sign painted by our man Richard Wilson.

I find this to be a slightly sad place. It seems unlikely now that a bustling railway station and inn operated here. The inn would have closed on its centenary, its sign made by a brilliantly over-qualified painter. There's no pleasing me really; I feel sad when new developments eat up our countryside, but I also feel sad when some such as the railway line here, are returned to nature. I suppose it's a matter of familiarity and time.

I opened up the boot of my car and put my wellies on. When I looked up, a herd of 40 odd ramblers had appeared from nowhere. They were being shepherded by a slightly harassed looking guide. They laid siege to the old station, now a private house, taking photographs from all possible angles. It would have been a very bad time for the occupant to step out of the shower without first placing a towel within easy reach. In the knowledge that there was only one footpath nearby, and with some trepidation, I asked a straggler which way they were heading. He informed me they were railway ramblers, following the now disused line from Mold to Penyffordd.

The bridge at Llong, as now seems the rule, was much more substantial when viewed up close and personal a` *pied*, paced up and down and generally caressed. A large central arch was complimented by a smaller one which was curiously high and dry. On the downstream side there was an old wall which looked as if it guided a flow of water, possibly to the wheel of a water mill. A memory was triggered from the deep cobweb-strewn recesses of my mind of trips to the nearby farm supplies warehouse to buy straw for my daughter Eira's pet rabbit. I'm sure it used to be referred to as Llong Mill. I used to enjoy driving home with a half bale of straw in the back of the car; it felt good, like I was some sort of micro-farmer.

I decided to stroll over to the current mill. A man was busy hauling bags of feed. I in a much less energetic fashion enquired if there was a water mill here at one time. He said no. The stonework was a flood defence feature. The name Llong Mill derived from the generic milled feed sense of the word, not specifically a water mill. It's so easy to make assumptions. My river-reading skills are clearly not the best. While following the Alun downstream, I'd failed to notice numerous leats and now I was seeing a leat when there was none. I'm going leat-crazy!

A few hundred yards toward the centre of the old flood plain, a tumulus is marked on my map. The Gold Cape exhibitions in Mold and Wrexham showed this as a Bronze Age burial mound excavated in the 1950s. I peered over the hedge expecting to see something resembling a burial mound, possibly topped with stone, but if it weren't for the location being mapped I would have passed this location un-noticed. A merest bump in the ground was all that remained. A fresh, neatly drilled crop went straight over the top of the mound, (if it possessed sufficient height for it still be called a mound).

The river Terrig flowed some distance behind me along the southern flank of the valley. Whatever stood here would have been pretty much slap bang in the middle of the flood plain, witnessed by the rounded pebbles at my feet.

I could well imagine a slightly raised peninsula here, overlooking the confluence of the Alun and the Terrig, long since obliterated by agriculture, erosion and time, watery wastes on either side, a point to make offerings to the water deities and a noble resting place for a Bronze Age big-wig.

Opposite The Old Inn a footpath leads through a field to the bridge over the Terrig on the Mold-Wrexham road. I paused for a second. Inside the Loggerheads Inn there is a copy of its Wilson painted sign on display. I wondered what happened to the sign from The Ship; I'd like to think it is safe and well and has pride of place in the building it was intended for, now a private house. This inn and the railway station would have stood on the flood plain side of the river, surely prone to inundation. I'm sure there is a quirk of history which explains their location.

Some months later, I was driving over the bridge at Llong, and there, directly opposite, against a hedge in the stonemason's garden, amidst a jumble of wood, rested a blue sign, looking in remarkably good condition, with big painted characters proclaiming "The Ship Inn."

The owner explained that it was *this* building that once housed the Ship Inn. Another wrong assumption: Llong isn't a big place, but I'd managed to read it totally back to front.

Its location makes perfect sense. A pre-railway era inn would surely have been located on the roadside, away from the flood plain. The owner has made enquiries if the Wilson painting is still in existence but so far has not been able to locate it. Maybe one day, with luck. The "Old Inn" house was possibly a later, railway-era watering hole?

The Terrig holds warm memories, as in the early 1990s I lived in Leeswood, at the top of the hill which the Terrig skirts. Occasionally on a summer's night, after an evening of merriment in Mold, I would pause at the bridge by the gates to Leeswood Hall and lie down on the wall looking up at the stars, the Terrig babbling below me. Those little soirees would have failed any risk assessment.

Rain-smudged footprints in the soft mud extended toward the bridge over the Terrig. Could this be Mr or Mrs Otter? I looked closely for the tell-tale webbing between the toes but it wasn't conclusive. I'm sure a better trained eye would have been able to give a definitive yay or nay. The tracks faded out along the bank. Otters are great wanderers. It is said they can range up to 30 miles depending on food supply. Dogs roam further than bitches. They can travel long distances over land to get from one watercourse to the next. A ledge at the side of the bridge provided another welcome wildlife corridor underneath the busy road. Otter numbers are thankfully on the increase, but one of the greatest threats to them today is from cars.

The Terrig had a hearty flow, the volume being virtually the same as the post-pilfered Alun. The saying that something can be greater than the sum of its parts is actually reversed for the Alun.

The Terrig is channelled, its banks built up and in places stone-lined, to speed it on its way. It felt remote here, easy to forget the nearby busy road. A brilliantly coloured male bullfinch sat plumped up on a branch, a robin followed my progress; their vivid colours stood out against the naked trees. The flow into the Alun formed a wonderful inverted "V" shaped confluence. There were more footprints

*1. The white gates at Leeswood Hall;*
*2. The Terrig just before she joins the Alun*

here – so many so that they criss-crossed in a Jackson Pollock style. It looked like a meeting point for the critters of the area. A bird carcass nearby looked like the remains of a fox kill. If the river was their highway, this was their service station. For me it was a dead end: I had to return the way I came and rejoin the Alun downstream.

A few days later, I popped down to the Golf Club to see if they would mind if I followed the course of the Alun across their land. As I walked toward the clubhouse with snow on the ground I thought I might get a frosty response (no pun). Far from it; the clubhouse was warm and inviting. A few people were having lunch; there was the satisfying chink of glasses. "No problem." I was given directions down the old railway line, so off I went to the Llong end of the course. The Alun does a sharp turn here around the periphery of the course. The steward in the club house mentioned it had been diverted at some time. I assumed this to be a minor change and that this must have been where it had taken place. I tried looking for an old river bed through the golf course but the landscape had been much manipulated, with raised areas for tees, drainage channels, etc. I followed the muddy melt water flow. Badger tracks led away in front of me. The course offered a change in habitat to the scrub on the opposite bank. There were plenty of nests in the managed trees. Sometime later I picked up *Mold Town and Country* by T. W. Pritchard which has a map of the Alun valley during the early Middle Ages (qualified with 'documented and likely sites'). The map shows various motte and bailey castle sites in the area, but what caught my eye was the dotted line labelled "Old course of the Alun?" which extended from this sharp deviation, onwards to Padeswood Pool. If the Alun had been diverted here, this would have been a significant change and raises many questions, the first being why? – Possibly this flood plain area was reclaimed for agriculture. It's not easy to confirm this on the ground. The golf course has been heavily landscaped and the Padeswood area is much affected by industrial activity. From Padeswood Pool the Alun would have joined Black Brook onward to reconnect with its present flow north of Hope. My map shows no Alun place names along Black Brook to confirm any earlier course. The house and farm at Bryn Alyn and Alyn Bank on the 'current' Alun were presumably named relatively recently.

I walked on top of the flood protection levee; throwing Golf balls which I found every now and again back on to fairway as thanks for free passage. I saw the Terrig intersection where I stood last week, from a much more comfortable lawned viewpoint. The Terrig was brown compared to the Alun, probably carrying peat from the marshy areas around Treuddyn. The two houses on the edge of the Mold-Wrexham dual carriageway looked much more tranquil from this direction. The white house nearer Mold had a channel of water leading to it, but not connected to the river. I wondered if this is a natural feature or if it was made for some long forgotten process. The map gave no clue. Little Egrets sometimes add a flash of white to the flooded fields here.

Not a soul on the course.

Then, snow, snow, snow. I was engulfed by horizontally driven snow from behind me, I hadn't noticed it coming. The wind picked up out of nowhere. I tried to shelter behind a tree but it was futile, the wind veered round and the cold soft snow found me. My gloves were once again stowed snug at home and my hands turned a violent shade of blue. Golfers obviously have better weather sense than I.

The snow was now building up and the visibility was dreamily low. A buzzard clumsily flapped between two trees, darkness in the light. Animal tracks on the bank were now covered up. I saw the gardens of Alyn Bank House softly undulating to the water's edge. Behind me there was a golden glow. I saw a manufactured landscape, with manicured lawns and ornamental bridges. I crossed arrow-straight drainage ditches. I felt like I was in a perfectly composed scene in a snow shaker. I had warmed up and didn't mind if this lasted for some time. It felt safe and comfortable. I wouldn't have been surprised if Mr Tumnes had strolled past. It didn't last, of course, but my return to reality was thankfully gentle. I always expect these occurrences to end with a shrill alarm clock. The snowfall ended and the clouds were blown on their way to reveal a bright blue sky.

I resumed the journey at Pontblyddyn, with my son Sion. On my last visit here with Sophia, we were hit by a squall of sleet, that most inconvenient weather form which finds any weakness in protective clothing and laughs at any attempt to take notes. We had made a hasty retreat. This time the skies were pretty clear. A flurry of small birds scattered quickly as we went down the path, too fast to identify them all, except for the usual tit suspects and a robin. We followed the river upstream, past the billiard-table lawned Golf course on the opposite bank. On our side rough scrub was pocked with vole activity and with lots of trees and perching points around, this looks like owl heaven. In between snow flattened reeds, the green shoots of early spring poked out of the soft mud.

**Black Gold**

Between the road and the river at Pontblyddyn, a small flat area of ground had a light dusting of snow but no vegetation. I drew my boot across the surface to reveal shale hardcore.

This site once housed a large industrial complex, a hive of activity, with two railway lines crossing the Alun, bringing in raw materials and carrying away finished products.

So what was it that once took place here that demanded such extensive works and infrastructure, but has left little trace on the ground or in the memory?

A short distance upstream at Mold, the banks of the Alun offered up gold in the form of the exquisite cape. This area coughed up gold in an altogether different form – "black gold", for it was a part of Flintshire's very own oil bonanza.

In the mid 1800s, a stone's throw away at Leeswood it was discovered that the already established coal reserves also contained a seam of a rare type of coal – "Cannel coal", from which oil could be distilled. Texas tea: right here in Flintshire.

The small area of shale would most likely be from the Pontblyddyn Coal and Oil works which occupied this site from 1860 to 1873.

Cannel coal is a hard, compact kind of bituminous coal. Its name maybe derives from "candle" because of the manner in which it burns. It was highly prized, as it could yield high profits when distilled into crude oil, paraffin and greases, etc.

The oil boom was, however, short-lived, the nature of Cannel coal is that it is found in thin seams and is quickly worked. The extent of the find was confined to within a couple of miles of the Leeswood area. At the same time the American oil industry took off, leading to imports of illuminating oils.

For twenty odd years oil overtook King Coal in this area. At its peak in 1865 some 150,000 tons of Cannel Coal were raised, the vast majority of it for use in more than 20 oil works which had sprung up in the Leeswood area alone. In 1851, the largest ever piece of Cannel, measuring approximately 8 by 14 feet was raised in Coed Talon. It was transported for display at the Great Exhibition at Crystal Palace.

I glanced at the O.S. map; I love the full title "ordnance" survey, derived from maps originally prepared under the master of ordnance to prepare the country in anticipation of a French invasion. Through the winter-beaten undergrowth I could see what looked like an old railway embankment, curving away from the present day roadside houses toward the Alun at Coppa Wood. The map showed another section to the south, running parallel to the Alun, and onwards to the Mold – Wrexham road. I picked up the route at the dingle intersection and came across the remains of a stranded rail cart, hidden in the trees and quietly decomposing. The old line, now grassed over, runs silently off behind the garage and up the Nant to Coed Talon. The line carried bricks and tiles as well as coal to the Mold – Denbigh line at Padeswood, where there was a tin plate works in addition to an oil plant. It's difficult for me to imagine today's sleepy Padeswood as it once was with heavy industry, a railway station and flat-capped workers clutching bottles of beer at the inn.

Christ church Pontblyddyn was built in 1836 to accommodate the spiritual needs of the sharply increased population when the Industrial Revolution spilled into these parts.

One of the chief protagonists in raising funds for the new church was the vicar of Mold, none other than the Reverend Clough of Mold Cape fame. He also built other churches in his parish, along with vicarages and schools.

A stroll through the graveyard gives a reminder of how hard life was and the human cost of the Industrial Revolution. A headstone commemorates "one of the eight who drowned in the flue pit colliery [on] December 15th 1864" – he was only 10 years old.

Pontblyddyn – a crossroads for who knows how long? Nant Brook leads here from the south carrying the A5104 and joining the Alun in a short valley. On the north bank just opposite, a gentle hill leads up to Coppa Wood; taking the road onward to Chester.

Offa's Dyke is generally accepted to end its northerly journey abruptly on an uphill stretch just short of Treuddyn village, some two miles to the south, heading towards the coast but not making it for whatever reason, possibly an early financial crisis or a sudden outbreak of peace, while Wat's Dyke passes just over a mile to the north.

A short distance before Offa's Dyke grinds to a halt, just after Llanfynydd, it bids farewell to the now dismantled railway to Coed Talon, which it has recently accompanied albeit on opposite sides of the valley from Ffrith. Means of passage generally take the easiest route, just as the B5101 sits squat atop the dyke for its penultimate stretch, the railway took the flat, though marshy land below the flank of Hope Mountain to Coed Talon. The line didn't stop there as back in the day it extended via Nant Brook to Pontblyddyn and further on to Padeswood via Coppa, neatly connecting with Wat's Dyke.

Could it be that a lost section of go-bween dyke, or more feasibly the natural features of the slopes of Hope Mountain, with marshy areas to the south and north of Pontblyddyn have formed a physical barrier which connected the two dykes for the journey north? This could possibly explain the sometime labelling of the final section of Wat's Dyke as Offa's Dyke. If old Offa had had access to a time machine, to take him to 1849, he could even, on production of a valid ticket, have travelled between the two dykes by train, had it not been for freight only!

This of course assumes that Wat's Dyke pre-dates Offa's Dyke, which is a matter of debate, but this seems likely as it is to the east of Offa's Dyke which would have been a later expansion of Offa's kingdom?

Whatever occurred with respect to any inter-connect, I'm sure Pontblyddyn saw many an incident in its position in the land between two dykes.

# 15. Big Country Houses

On a cold, snowy New Years Day I followed the footpath from Pontblyddyn village up behind the Bridge Inn which dates from 1758. On a bridge, a funky brass plaque, awarded in 1987, highlights work done by an angling club. This is no dull single typescript plaque, it is an illustrated work of art, interesting in its own right, but it is the text which caught my eye. The award was made for various improvements to the river, one of them being works to counter the effects of loss of water through the river bed. I thought we'd left the swallow holes well behind us, but clearly not. It really is amazing how the Alun continues to flow, despite being regularly held up and shaken down. I wondered where the aqua pilfered from this particular location ended up. I noticed that Plas Teg was represented in the corner of the plaque, but Hartsheath, which is closer, was not

A swirl of snow chilled my face; I zipped my coat up tightly to my chin and a flurry of LBJs scattered ahead of me. I entered a lovely wooded area, passing the mill house to the right; the Corn Mill itself no longer stands. The path led upwards, away from the river onto the brow of a hill where a buzzard hopped onto a branch on

*1. Pontblyddyn art-plaque; 2. Damselfly*

the opposite side of field. I passed the solid mass of Hartsheath. This high ground surrounded by marsh must have had strategic importance before the surrounding wetlands were tamed.

Hidden away, overshadowed by it's more famous neighbour; I get the feeling that's how they like it, surrounded by trees, visible only in short glimpses from the Mold-Wrexham road.

Originally "Plas yn Hersedd," the seat of the Lloyd family, the twelfth noble tribe of Wales, Hartsheath's deeds date back to 1616.

The signposts for the path were good at first, but if they continued to be so, then I managed to evade them successfully; I followed the features on my map and rejoined the Alun at the bridge near Plas Teg.

The first recorded occupants of the Plas Teg site were the Ithel family, who rose up in Glyndŵr's rebellion. The classic Jacobean country house we see now has a colourful history. It was built in 1610 for Sir John Trevor, who in the Civil War, sided with the Parliamentarians. This resulted in him being stripped of his position as surveyor of the king's Navy, but did not stop Plas Teg being plundered by a troop of Parliamentarians in 1645, unaware of Sir John's loyalties in this predominantly royalist area. On the highly recommended tours, they tell of Cromwell's men riding their horses up the wide staircases. It is said that during the Second World War, American soldiers billeted at Plas Teg fled the building after hearing the ghostly footsteps of horses on the landing.

Plas Teg has had many incarnations. "Hanging Judge Jeffries" is reputed to have cemented his notoriety here when it was used as a court. In 1685, after Monmouth's failed attempt to overthrow James II, Judge Jeffries issued harsh sentences, including many executions. Other uses include that of an auctioneer's store and my particular favourite, a 1970's discotheque. Boogying under the 'hanging beam' to Sister Sledge may hold warm memories for someone in the locality, possibly unaware of its grisly past.

Plas Teg has been saved from dereliction by Mrs Cornelia Bailey, who has poured her extensive energy and expertise into restoring the very fabric of the house. Stand in the Great Hall, and imagine a river flowing through it; that was her starting point.

It's big on the ghost-hunting scene and does undoubtedly have an 'other worldly' feel about it, even on a bright Sunday afternoon.

As I looked up at the house from the Alun I was reminded of the guided tour story of a burial mound being unearthed when the Mold-Wrexham road was widened in the 1970s (demolishing the north lodge in the process). I have often wondered what the domed structure at the edge of the road is and if it was in any way connected to the burial. It is a substantial building, now door-less, grassed over. It is directly between the house and the river, so I wondered if it was on the same level as my usual architectural deductions – something to do with drains.

It turned out to be a one-time ice house used to store game, though of course, as is the way with old buildings, there is talk of an underground passage connecting it to the house. Game killed in the autumn would be stored here before being taken to the main house. At one time the estate ran to around 2,000 acres, today it's more like two and a half.

The footpath from the Alun towards Plas Teg joins the road adjacent to a pair of handsome stone dressed and capped gateposts. I sat here a while remembering a newspaper article which reported a distressed motorist reporting to police that she had knocked down a woman dressed all in black as she walked out in front of her on this stretch of road. A police search found no evidence of any accident. The account triggered responses from other people who gave details of similar experiences. The woman is said to be the ghost of the 16 year old daughter of Sir John, who had fallen in love with the son of a local farmer. On her way to elope, she went to retrieve her jewels which she had hidden in a well; she lost her footing,

*Plas Teg*

fell in and drowned. Her beau, thinking she had deserted him, hung himself. Their ghosts are said to wander the area, looking for each other.

I followed the main road until I was square on to the front of Plas Teg, its grey stonework transitions to yellow in some of the central and upper areas. The four domed cupolas are surmounted by bell towers, each having four further stone corner pieces. These are pure indulgence, a statement, justified by their beauty alone, serving no purpose other than to look splendid. Some of the window panes are false – given away by their black colouring – for they contain no glass and were built during a time when windows were taxed, when even Plas Teg had its budget.

The avenue of lime trees leading to the front gates is now redundant, the furthermost pair looked particularly sad, marooned on their central reservation island. The trees are the only indicator of what must have been a very grand driveway to this very imposing building.

I doubled back along the road to catch a glimpse of Y Fferm at Pontblyddyn. Initials in a cobbled path are said to relate to a romantic entwinement in 1642; the manor house is thought to date back even earlier.

Pontblyddyn Cricket Ground, sitting in a clearing in the trees next to a sweep in the river on the valley floor, seems like an unlikely spot for cricket. It must be tricky on the drainage front. I could well imagine spending a luxurious time-fat day here, the slow-fast game interspersed with gentle clapping, condensation running down a glass, and a hazy sun setting behind the trees.

I leave Hartsheath behind me and follow a path on the east bank. The grass here is kept very short by a herd of sheep and almost looks like a golf course, except for their doings. The Kennedy Space centre style chimney stack of the cement works looms in the distance. Red lights announce its presence to the circling jet undergoing flight trials.

I crossed Black Brook on the eastern side of the valley floor, over a dodgy wooden bridge with some of the wooden slats missing. As I headed further south the mood changed, the stiles were not user-friendly, rounded wooden rungs were slippery underfoot and barbed wire had to be eased out of the way.

A sole goose flew overhead as I

rounded a bend; I saw hundreds more through the trees. I tried to pass them quietly keeping low and close to the river. They shuffled, sprinted then erupted skyward, their combined noise like a jet engine. They honked loudly and circled before selecting a new sanctuary downstream.

Goldfinches ahead provided flashes of yellow in the gloom, flitting and tinkling. Hope Mountain to my right was snow-covered, dyke-straddled and silent; she is my companion in marking the seasons, the solstices and failed attempts at seeing the Aurora Borealis. On her shoulder the sacred waters of Waun y Llyn, the valley of the lake, are secreted, the nearby ribboned wishing tree imbued with hopes.

From my house I can ascend to Waun y Llyn in a brisk forty five minute walk, though I'm more likely to take a few hours as I allow the view to soak in, and sometimes the rain to soak me. To walk slowly through the ever changing landscape is a joy; the mountain has serenaded me with blistering heat, horizontal rain, waist high snow and cheek-stinging hail. I enjoy the winters as much as the summers, moving at the speed of a glacier I have observed splay-

legged buzzards pulling up worms, early morning foxes dancing on the frozen ground to summon up a breakfast, disorientated barn owls forced to hunt in daylight when offerings are thin on the ground. These encounters cause me to count my blessings, to thank providence. The mountain shares my clumsy steps with badgers and hares, rabbits and stoats. On a summers dawdle I sat on a stile-throne on her flank when a yellow-mohicaned goldcrest (dryw eurben), the UK's smallest bird, landed on a branch a yard or so above my head. On another occasion the sound of a mechanical rat-tat-tat caused me to stop and search for its source – presumably a

*The cement works at Padeswood*

nearby farm thought I, moving stealthily upward until I was rewarded for a glorious hour by a great spotted woodpecker rapping its metallic love notes on an electricity pylon to a suitor who was responding in a lower tone from a nearby telegraph pole. A happy hour of premium entertainment ensued, I have to disagree with Lene Lovich – the best things in life are free and I'm delighted to enjoy them with the birds and bees. On a late spring walk just over the summit, I was similarly cheered by an adult kestrel training its young to hunt, I watched on as they took turns to circle and hover from their tree-top launch-pad.

The lake sits in a bowl, a belly button

*Hope mountain: old and new*

of the Celts, a high place where time is slowed. A walks decision point, do I return to Hope or go onwards to Llanfynydd, a friendly village with rustic charm and excellent sustenance? And then further again to Cymau for a full all-you can-walk-banquet mountain circuit in the long days of summer?

I'm not aware of any myths or mountain witches, sleeping dragons or Quaker revelations concerning Hope Mountain although it has the feel of the high places about it, a place of total retreat, and a solid accomplice in midsummer bivy bag sunrises.

I arrived at the old gravel quarry, now a quiet 30-acre lake where ducks and geese frolic. Large deposits of sand and gravel were laid down in the middle Alun valley after the last glacial period. They were extracted in the Fagl Lane area up to 2004 using a floating dredger and barges. At the time of writing there are ambitious and exciting plans to build a Roman Fort and Iron Age farmstead on the old quarry site in a first-century environment. Early O.S. maps of this area show an avenue of standing stones, I've walked the area where they stood, hoping to rediscover maybe a single one hidden in a hedge, but found nothing, possibly they are now employed as lintels in nearby houses or as gateposts to the fields, who knows how much history has been lost, and what remains to be found.

Approaching Hope the Alun had a melancholy air about her; she flowed full, yet almost in silence. Branches of gnarled crack willow were cast out Halloween-style looking sickly, in pain. Brittle, sap-meagre desiccated boughs waited for spring, but received no warm welcome today. The river looked abandoned, left to its own devices. Signs, roughly nailed to gothic trees, proclaimed "private fishing – poachers will be prosecuted".

This area in summer is totally different, it really comes alive; it's one of my favourite walks. I recall an early June walk where, within seconds of taking to the path, there was a flurry of movement in the grass a few inches in front of my foot. I waited a second; having only seen a dash of darker green which I thought was a frog. Just to my right I saw a tail disappear over a low wall, which I thought could be a lizard, albeit a large one. I looked over the wall which lined a small stream. In the flow I caught a glimpse of a straightening out 'S', which I now guessed was an eel, until I saw it slide up the opposite bank into the field; a glorious grass snake, beautiful olive green with black slashes.

On the same walk I saw a kingfisher, masses of shimmering metallic-blue damsel flies, great crested grebes, a pair of bullfinches, and 80 or so greylag geese. The birdsong was so rich, there must have been much more waiting to be discovered in the trees. I've also seen a pair of young stoats here, frolicking in the undergrowth at the water's edge. One of them stood upright meerkat-like directly in front of me as if posing for a photograph. If the batteries in my camera had not failed me, I would gladly have obliged.

This is a great area, on a warm dry afternoon, with time to spare, to find some sun baked soil and kick off the boots, to listen to the feet sigh as the heat is released and the breeze circulates through extended toes. Even better, to find a secluded spot and slip in to the warm shallow water for a liberating skinny dip, a definite step up from the humble paddle, better than any 'luxury' spa. 'Freedom' as Cicero said 'is man's natural power of doing what he pleases, so far as he is not prevented by force or law'.

*Autumn Alun near Hope*

# 16. Live in Hope; Die in Exile

At Hope, snow covered the bridge carrying the road to Mold, an older, solid-looking narrower bridge runs parallel, its keystones seeming to defy gravity, held in place only by thin cracked mortar. Under the new bridge animal tracks led to territory-marking spraint on a concrete block. I considered doing the "smells like jasmine tea" test for otter doings, but with insufficient time having elapsed since breakfast, I satisfied myself that, beyond reasonable doubt, it was indeed of otter...

The river under the road here is an unseen wildlife corridor, a separate transport system, oblivious to the rules of the Highway Code and mechanised conveyances. The soft mud on the banks records the movements of numerous creatures. It's an overgrown place where a tail disappearing under a tree could be a squirrel or mink and the flash of blue above could be a Kingfisher or Jay (*sgrech y coed* – the screech of the woods).

Near Hope railway station a slope provided a happy diversion for a group of youngsters, the snow having momentarily enticed them away from electronica to the fashioning of wholesome improvised sledges, on which they launched themselves downward with wild abandon. Although the sight was a heart-warming one, my council estate upbringing told me that in the blink of an eye, they could re-form into a crack artillery division. I chose a stealthy route close to the river and passed by unnoticed, like a thief in the night.

I heard the bells of St Cynfarch's, its tower now visible from the river. It is

*St Cynfarch's, Hope*

thought to be one of the earliest Christian sites in North Wales, possibly dating back to the sixth century.

The church is well worth the small diversion, located as it is on a small hill at the heart of the village (Hope is old English, meaning "enclosed land in a marsh").

The church sits on a gentle slope facing the whale back of Hope Mountain. Sheep graze under the large copper beech near the front entrance. Ancient yews look down upon the Red and White Lions, offering their alternative sustenance. Two old millstones are built into the south wall; from an age when recycling was the norm. The transmitter mast on Hope Mountain used to bother me, crowning the summit with its scaffold-like utilitarian framework. No 'Christ the Redeemer' for us to admire; no simple illuminated cross or sculpture as a mask or diversion. A couple of winters ago a light was left on, presumably in the small service building at its base, which for a few successive evening walks drew my attention to the summit, marking, in the cows belly blackness, the transition between earth and sky. I imagined a tall figure in a hooded cloak holding a lamp above his head in the manner of a 1970s album cover, casting a protective light over Hope village. On another, idle, dreamy, starrygazey twilight evening the mast morphed into the rigging of a pirate ship, appearing Marquez-like over the skyline. I'm now completely at ease with the arrangement of mountain furniture.

Parts of the current church structure date back to the twelfth century. Internally the structure is no less interesting: from the main door the entrant walks through the base of the tower to a set of steps to the floor of the main church, which is almost at eye level. The tower was at one time a separate structure – this can be seen in the differing external stonework. A leaflet found inside advises "the tower was built as an independent structure in three stages to allow for the settlement of a superincumbent mass of stone upon the foundation and was joined to the Nave between 1520 and 1560"; pure poetry. Despite this care, there was structural movement, albeit several centuries later. In 2000 a major restoration was carried out. To my eyes this has blended a modern functioning church within an ancient structure with some style.

A memorial to the Trevor family of Plas Teg can be seen on the south wall of the side chapel. Another benefactor of St Cynfarch's was Margaret Beaufort (as at Mold). A light and modern wooden altar sits nearby, skilfully crafted into beautiful lines from oak removed during the 2000 restoration.

Hope has a brief mention in the Domesday Book, giving its location on the river Alyn. Hope Hall (demolished 1974) and Hope Mountain (still very much standing) at 1085ft also appear. In the past, fairs were held in Hope on Shrove Tuesday, May 10th, August 12th and October 27th.

From my house, I can gaze up at two former defensive structures from feistier times and reflect on being born into a historically rare period of peace.

To the right through naked winter trees I can see the ruins of Caergwrle castle, the last of who knows how many battlements topping that hill.

To the left I spy Caer Estyn Hill, the calf of Hope Mountain, its tree-covered slopes concealing the now, sadly, (partially-quarried) Iron Age hill fort. The quarrying did, however, deliver a fantastic sight on several consecutive clear autumn nights, when cosmic orbits conspired to cause a rising full moon to appear in perfect harmony, for several joyful minutes, with the scallop cut out of the hill. It almost looked like resurrected quarried material making a break for freedom. A saw-tooth "V" shaped notch in the tree line on its western flank gives passage to Wat's Dyke. A path leads off from this point over the shoulder of the hill toward the quarry bite, its line when emphasised by snow being of an uncanny aero dynamicity that would grace any sports car or TGV.

Sarn Bridge crosses the Alun below Hope station, replacing the stepping stones which were in use here until 1886. *Sarn* is Welsh for causeway, a reference to the marsh which would have covered the valley floor. Today the river flows fast over its gravel bed. There is some sand toward the bank where branches dip into the flow and are coated with ice. The river runs parallel to the railway track; a train passes carrying Saturday day-trippers to Liverpool in search of city things and possibly, bowls of delicious Lobsgows.

Upstream of the Sarn Bridge the river is sandwiched between two footpaths which are glorious for mid-summer sunset strolls. Quiet curves invite a pause to enjoy the fading of the light; bright orange skies turn gently to blue. Moths zig and zag above the sweet- smelling choke of purple Balsam flowers. Bats even more agile swoop and twist, while the laser-straight blur of a blue kingfisher cuts low across the dilly-dallying lazy flow. Either side a tree tunnel of darkness forms, over belly-flopping fly-chasing fish. I stay until the mist begins to form on the field below the railway station, until the cold of night licks my forearms, the rustle in the undergrowth and hoo-hoo of a tawny owl announces its shift change on the bank.

An ordnance survey map dated 1927 shows the Alun below the bridge did not always run so straight here. A blue curve, a displaced if shallow ox-bow lake, rests to the east of the railway line indicating a realignment to ease the passage of iron horses.

I continued, like a negative against the snow, wildlife fleeing well in advance of me. Leaving Hope, the Alun takes an unexpected ninety-degree turn to the right. The line of trees which to this point accompanied rail and river, continues on its linear axis to a cutting which conveys the railway south, the Alun has to take the long way around this guardian hill, forming the shape of a letter C, before reacquainting itself with the railway a short distance ahead, where they share the confines of the narrow valley between Caer Estyn and Castle Hill.

And so I arrived at the linguistic car crash which is Caergwrle. When I first saw the village sign many years back, I have to admit I thought the local pronunciation of "Caegirlie" must be an Anglicisation of a Welsh form. The story is more complex and reflective of the border location we are in."Caer" is Welsh meaning castle or fort. The gwrle is thought to be a Welsh form of the old English "corley" from crane and "leah" from clearing or meadow. There are variations on this theme, but this seems the most common, so as far as I can see; the name stems from two languages, and has a pronunciation all of its own.

The picturesque Packhorse Bridge (*Y Bont Pynfarch*) dissects the C of the Alun; a plaque commemorates its rebuilding, after the floods of November 2000.

"The Packhorse Bridge dates from the mid-seventeenth century and is associated with Squire Ellis Young, of Bryn Iorcyn manor. It incorporates seven arches to reduce the impact of the flow of the river during periods of flooding. Packhorse bridges were generally of a narrow

*The Packhorse Bridge*

construction and the Caergwrle example originally contained two triangular recesses, in the parapet walls, for pedestrians who might meet a packhorse train whilst crossing the bridge. The low parapets were intended to allow the passage of bulging packs slung on each side of mules and packhorses. It is probably the oldest bridge to span the river Alyn and is one of the finest examples of its type in Wales."

The bridge suffered severe damage in the floods of 2000, despite those many arches (I can only count six by the way; it must have lost one over the years). Full marks for the restoration, and whether there are six or seven arches, they gracefully straddle the valley.

The plaque also highlights the importance of this bridge on the Bala-Chester packhorse trail. It's easy to cross the Alun at Bridge End or Fagl Lane these days, but historically this must have been a crucial crossing for traders, as indicated by the need for passing points.

In "Following Kings and Gunpowder Plotters – A walk from Shrewsbury Abbey to St Winefride's Well Holywell" by Raymond Roberts, Mr. Roberts describes his attempt to corroborate accounts of a pilgrimage by Guy Fawkes between these two points. His conclusion is that Fawkes never visited Holywell, although some of his fellow conspirators did; hence the title. What he did very much achieve was to come up with a fantastic 80-mile route between the two points. This is his own route, not a step-by-step historically accurate way, following "public footpaths, bridleways, river banks, canal towpaths, country lanes, drovers trails and roman roads….it passes ancient castles, abbeys, fine churches and not a few inns."

Many other routes, both historical and modern, including the Wat's Dyke Way, cross over the Packhorse Bridge. Sitting in a quiet corner of Caergwrle, it's no longer a question of needing to come via this way, but one of aesthetics, history and joy. His route follows the Alun from its end point at the Dee to Rossett, from Caergwrle it wends to Llanfynydd by way of Bryn Yorkin Lane.

Another day and another diversion brought me to *Hidden Highways of North Wales* by R. J. A. Dutton, a collection of 10 walks, one of which includes the Packhorse Bridge, a photo of which is titled "Pont y Delyn" and notes it was also recorded as Pont y Dorlan.

With his book in hand, on a tangentially inspired walk, I followed the old Packhorse Trail along Fellows Lane from the bridge in the direction of Chester. As I crossed Wat's Dyke on the shoulder of Caer Estyn I read: "Buried deep under the grassy surface are the cobble stones of the road which is three metres wide. These cobbles were laid in the 17th century to re-instate the trail that was showing considerable signs of wear and tear from the continual strings of packhorses".

This is the pure line of uncanny aero dynamicity which I thought was some sort of accident of recent history, skirting the perimeter of the Bronze Age hill fort, but the reality goes back centuries. From the highest point of the path, dead ahead, the twin grain silo's at Dodleston came into view, with Chester directly behind them. Those traders were on a mission to get their wares to market ASAP and in pre-enclosure times that would have meant keeping their route as near as possible to a straight line. On an early morning walk here a 'squirrel' approached me head on. It turned at ninety degrees to the path, its stretched-limo body puzzling me until its black paint-dipped tail identified it as a stoat.

The footpath over the bridge connecting the steep-sided hills on each side is now little used; the gardens at the back of the former Derby Arms stand empty.

This area once had an array of industries. A forge produced industrial and agricultural tools. The leat which flows under the packhorse bridge would have fed Caergwrle saw mill, the remains of which stands a short distance downstream, obscured by trees; it operated until 1928. The 1871 census showed "a very successful timber business employing 16 men, amongst them woodcutters, sawyers and timber measurers. They made fencing, gates, wheelbarrows, agricultural items and pit props for the local mines". There were three water-powered corn mills in Caergwrle – the first recorded date is to be found in a Ministers account from 1349 which details the costs of a new mill.

On the right of the river stood Caergwrle Brewery, taking advantage of an ample supply of spring water. It is now an area of residential housing.

A plaque on a nearby wall reads:

*"The area adjacent to the Derby Arms used to be the site of the famous Caergwrle Brewery which was founded in 1861 by William Lassell the Younger, the son of an amateur English astronomer. A partnership was subsequently formed with Septimus Sharman from Northampton and Lassell and Sharman Ltd. was floated as a limited liability company in 1897.The Brewery supplied many local public houses with beer until 1945 when it was acquired by Burtonwood Brewery and closed down. The building was later used as paint works and then as graphite works before it was dismantled in the 1990s".*

The Castle looms large over Caergwrle in this area of borders. When I drive the six miles from Hope to work, I cross Wat's Dyke, then the border into England and back into Wales. A short distance to the south Flintshire becomes Wrexham; Offa's Dyke lies just over Hope Mountain.

Claims have long been staked to "The Middle Country" or "The Lands Between" – "*Y Berfeddwlad*", this part of which strategically overlooks the fertile Cheshire plain. The Caer Estyn hill fort dates back to 750 BC. Caergwrle Castle Hill, on the opposite side of the Alun has a defensive structure thought to date back to 250 AD. The entrance to Nant y Ffrith valley where the Romans mined lead lies a short distance to the south. In times gone by when the area was heavily wooded the rivers would have been the highways of the region.

Wat's Dyke and Offa's Dyke were built by the Mercians to protect their boundaries with Wales. The Normans after 1066 controlled the lands through the Marcher lords. But it was from the mid-thirteenth century that events occurred which would shape the history of Wales to the present day. When Llywelyn ap Gruffudd refused to pay homage to the new English ruler, King Edward I, he and his brother Dafydd regained control of the area in 1262. Llywelyn was declared Prince

1. *The well at Caergwrle Castle;*
2. *Caergwrle castle*

of Wales; Dafydd, miffed at losing out to his elder brother formed an alliance with Edward.

In 1277, King Edward invaded, pushing Llywelyn back to the west of the river Conwy. Dafydd was rewarded with lands around Hope and Caergwrle, where he built the castle.

After 5 years Dafydd increasingly felt unfairly treated under English law. In 1282 Dafydd attacked the English garrison at Hawarden Castle, triggering a rebellion against the colonial castles throughout Wales. Llywelyn had no option but to take the lead, once more fighting alongside his brother.

Edward gathered a massive force. When he arrived at Caergwrle, he found that Dafydd had partly demolished his own castle and blocked the well to slow the advance.

Llywelyn was killed in a skirmish; Dafydd was not so lucky. He was captured alive and convicted of high treason, becoming the first nobleman in Britain to be hung, drawn and quartered. He was dragged to Shrewsbury for betraying the King, hung until almost dead for homicide, disembowelled for sacrilege and beheaded for plotting against the King. His head was sent to the Tower of London, while his quartered remains were distributed across England.

Caergwrle Castle was given to Edward's wife Eleanor and the area became known as Queen's Hope. Work began on rebuilding the castle but was abandoned after a fire in 1283.

It was a very bad time to be a Welshman in these parts, with land being allocated to English settlers and the indigenous Welsh expelled. A Welshman's head was worth 12d to raiding parties from the English castles.

In 1400 Owain Glyndŵr, a nobleman, rebelled against the harsh restrictions imposed on the Welsh and was declared Prince of Wales by his countrymen. He gained much support and attacked many English garrisons including Hope. The rebellion lasted 15 years, the longest in the whole history of the British Empire.

A plaque on the White Lion Inn at Hope reads:

*"On February 22nd 1403 forces loyal to Owain Glyndŵr, the reigning Prince of Wales, attacked and burned this town, thus liberating it from the forces of Henry IV".*

A path leads up the steep slope from the village to the castle. The area in front of the castle is now overgrown with bracken, photos from the heyday of tourism for the castle show Edwardian ladies in their finery stood on well manicured lawns, the castle rising above them. Crowds of people sit relax and take pleasure in picnics. The most striking difference is the absence of trees, which gives more emphasis to the castle.

The east wall and north tower still stand tall, while between them the defences have been razed. Some of the remaining pillars of the east tower have beautifully carved feet; an archway leading from the tower toward the main hall existed until recent times. In the castle itself the remains of an oven can be seen as well as the large well.

On this late autumn day, the trees on Hope Mountain still retain some red and yellow colouring. I see Bryn Iorcyn manor standing on a small plateau much higher than the castle; it's not often a castle is so closely overlooked.

I reflected on the current castle situation: it is open to all, a very welcome state of affairs. Some abuse this privilege;

I saw empty bottles, discarded fireworks and a camp fire. The tree covering now pretty much hides the castle away, giving the opportunity for unseen mischief and also depriving the populace of a fantastic view. I'm all in favour of tree planting, but possibly some judicious thinning out of the trees at the top would be beneficial: an arboreal tonsure perhaps? Dare I say the arch could also be rebuilt, giving back some romanticism?

## Caergwrle Bowl

Another find which gives weight to the Alun having been a greater river in pre-mining times is the Caergwrle 'bowl'. The incomplete and broken bowl was probably deliberately placed near the Alun, which at that time would have been an important water-way linking this area to the river Dee and the coast.

Found in 1823, in a field near the castle, it is a unique votive model boat from the Bronze Age. It is made from shale from Dorset, tin from Cornwall and gold from Ireland; this again tells a story of extensive trade links. The stamped gold foil on the rim of the bowl represents warriors' shields, while the zigzag decorations at the base are waves. There is also a pair of Oculi ('eyes') at both ends of the boat, which probably acted as a charm to ward off calamity at sea.

The composition of the gold shows it dates from around 3,200 years ago and is similar in age to the Gold Cape; a rich time for this area. Once again, as in the case of the Cape found some 10 years later, we are indebted to the British Museum for carrying out restoration work to the bowl in 1912. The bowl is now further re-conserved and on display in the National Museum of Wales in Cardiff. When I visited, there was also a modern and funky audio visual art installation by Sean Harris in which he depicted the 'bowl' being used to transport warriors from Ireland to Wales.

# 17. Spa Town

The bridge at Bridge End is gracefully dual-arched in warm stone and carries an 1838 inscription. Prior to its construction, the river here was crossed by means of a ford, located just below the fantastic weir.

An information board tells of the weir being built probably in the late nineteenth century and of the mill producing one of the worlds's first self- raising flours. It later also provided electricity to the Rhyddyn estate. A photo shows the mill in its latter years. In 1968 the shell of the mill building which was then been used for storage was converted into the fine private residence we see today. It continues to be occupied by the Parsonage family who kindly invited me in and lent me numerous photos and details concerning its history.

Bridge End is a great tranquil space for some water therapy, just sitting quietly by the river, listening, looking, thinking and more often, not thinking. Sections of millstones are built into the retaining walls of the garden, which has been tastefully landscaped on the site of some of the former mill buildings.

One October day I saw a large fish leaping below the weir. It was much bigger than anything I'd seen previously on the Alun. In the shade of the trees it looked brown rather than silver, more like a sea trout than a Salmon. A week previously, a fisherman had stood at the top of the fish ladder watching for Salmon which he confirmed were found in the Alun. I'd been sceptical of their presence, not having had a sniff of one over the previous few years of Alun-bonding. I took over his position at the top of the ladder, waited patiently in a cross-eyed eternity, but saw nothing further. I've been told stories of

*The Alun in spate at Bridge End*

people gathering on the bridge in years gone by to watch fish ascend the weir; it could be that the re-furbished fish ladder now allows unseen passage – a hidden success story?

One sighting I made here was beautiful but un-welcome. While gazing downstream one late afternoon in May, I saw what first appeared to be a black cat, walking away from me, on the stones below the mill wall. Its furry tail caught my attention; it would have been an unusual spot to see a cat. It went out of view behind a boulder, and then re-appeared further downstream. It straightened up, performed a perfect dive into the water and was gone, clearly not a cat. I considered if it could be a young otter, but its furry tail drew me to conclude it was a mink. I can't deny it was a captivating sight, but at the same time the mink will probably be the reason I won't see a water vole on the Alun. Introduced from Alaska and Canada for the fashion industry these voracious hunters can squeeze themselves in to the water vole's small burrows.

The road past the old mill leads up Rhyddyn Hill overlooking the now romantically overgrown ornamental portcullis entrance to Caergwrle Spa. A useful sign gives the following:

"The old Caergwrle Spa site is situated behind this board. Its natural spring waters were noted for their health-giving properties and attracted hordes of visitors in the early years of the twentieth century.

Many arrived here by train and there was plenty of accommodation available in local Inns and guest houses. The Bottling Works which was housed in the red Ruabon brick building just beyond the main gateway was still producing 14,000 bottles of spa water a day in the 1920s.

The Spa fell into disuse in the 1930's although it had once played an important role in the economy and culture of the locality".

I followed a lane along my old friend the Wat's Dyke path, running past the bottling works and Rhyddyn Hall, which dates back to the seventeenth century. The springs on the estate have long been renowned for their medicinal properties. Thomas Pennant wrote: "adjoining the Alyn, are two springs, strongly impregnated with salt; which, in dry weather, used to be the great resort of pigeons to pick up the hardened particles. These were formerly used as a remedy in scorbutic cases... the effect was purging, griping and sickness at the stomach, which went off in a few days, and then produced a good appetite. Dr. Short gives an instance of a woman in a deplorable situation from a scurvy, who was perfectly restored by the use of these springs."

But it was at the start of the twentieth century that the waters were developed commercially. A change of owner at the hall, coinciding with the growth of the railways, allowed the springs to become a major tourist attraction. A pump house was constructed, the hall was converted into a hotel, and there were grounds with riverside walks, a bandstand and a bowling green, as well as an entertainment pavilion. The area became a Mecca for day-trippers from Liverpool and Birkenhead. Large numbers of people came to visit the spa and Caergwrle Castle, or to enjoy one of the many publicised walks in the area.

One of the documents Mr. Parsonage kindly lent me was a booklet entitled "Rhyddin Hall – Park Spa – Descriptive Particulars and Analyses of the Waters"

published in 1903 which contains reports by "various eminent chemists" which highly praise the waters. "I have made an analysis of water taken from three wells at Caergwrle and find them all to contain considerable quantities of saline matter, which will have therapeutic value...the water could undoubtedly be used with beneficial results for the same disorders that are treated at Harrogate" states H. gripper Esq., F.C.S. While "my investigations prove these springs to be of a remarkable character...natural medicinal waters of a very valuable kind" writes T. Williams F.C.S.

A leaflet advertising Caergwrle Spa

*The bottling works from the castle in de-cluttered times*

complete with an illustration of a Welsh Lady carrying a tray of bottles of mineral water (trade Mark "Girlie") describes Rhyddin (sic) Hall as a "first class hotel, sumptuously furnished. Close to is the large tea pavilion on a terrace fronting the river fitted with stage and retiring rooms. The bowling green is one of the finest and largest in wales and is forty-five yards square. A short distance away is the bungalow and bandstand. Pleasant walks run by the side of the stream and in the woods".

The depression of the 1930s, an increase in the cost of rail tickets and changing times brought an end to the spa: the other attractions most definitely remain, gloriously crowd-free.

Rhyddyn Hall is now a private dwelling. Who knows, the vicissitudes of time may one day lead to the waters being taken once more. When the last ounce of joy has finally been squeezed out of flying, when the enforced striptease and overbearing commercialism of airports have finally become too much, long-time mothballed UK attractions may flourish once more.

As Caergwrle fades behind me, I ponder over another borrowed item from Mr. Parsonage – an official guide to Caergwrle which extends a cordial invitation to the "Gem of Lovely North Wales." It's most definitely a gem in my eyes and, at the appropriate time, I would be happy to comply with the saying "live in Hope, die in Caergwrle."

Passing the hall, a big vicious-looking Alsatian came charging towards me. Luckily an unseen master called, stopping it in its salivating tracks. The path continued high above the river. It was surprisingly rustic, the semi-urban location betrayed only by the sound of trucks and trains hidden by the trees on the opposite side of the valley. Near to Cefn y Bedd, I heard the river falling over the weir at the old Hope Paper Mill, unseen on the valley floor.

I decided to try to get a better view; the way down was very steep and slippery. I devised a plan; there was a tree conveniently located half way down, so I aimed for it, in theory halving the problem. Gravity had a different plan for me: I skidded past the tree on a wave of wet leaves and mud; with an outstretched arm I just managed to grasp it. The tree bent, slowing me down, it groaned, as it went past its elastic limit, then snapped. I continued on my journey downward, my trajectory being such that I went A over T fully utilising my nose to plough a furrow through the icy leaf mould. I opened my eyes, disappointed that I was not in a 'Romancing the Stone' style compromising position with Kathleen Turner. I was, I conceded, where I wanted to be, though this was never an option for getting there.

The large weir is no longer functional, an opening having being cut through it to allow fish to pass. The weir diverted water to the paper mill, first mentioned in 1811, which had replaced an earlier rope works on the site. By 1903 the site was being used in the production of "Vim" scouring powder using silica from Minera. Production ceased by 1915.

A large pool in the marshy hinterland above the weir, surrounded by fallen trees, was I decided, a perfect spot for otters. There should be plenty of snacks for them here: fish (lots of small trout), crustaceans, ducks, frogs and possibly even eels and water voles. I sat against a tree trunk, confused a squirrel which would have very much liked to have scampered up that particular tree, and successfully avoided any local otters. I determined henceforth to not mention otters, a bit like Shakespearian actors and the 'Scottish play'.

The fields above the valley were crisp snow-white. A gentle mist made the landscape soft, fuzzy, impressionist. It felt warm, even though it was just above freezing. I walked slowly, soaking up the atmosphere. The heavy snow had deposited branches of green across paths; orange brown scars on the trunks above highlighted where they had been torn away, as if a giant machete had sliced them off. In a bank at the side of the path, dirty brown trails showed which of the many front doors of a badger sett were in use.

Hope Mountain wore a warm yellow-orange mountain spirit halo. Big Turner brush strokes of yellow, white and grey were slashed across the sky, fading upward into pure blue, from which a banker's bonus of stars shone. As the final curve of the sun slipped down out of sight, the cold of the snow clawed at my feet and cheeks. Warmth reverted to cold in the final play of the sun's daily cycle.

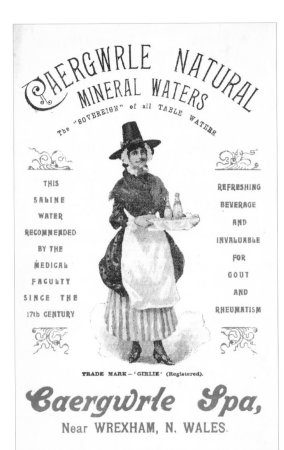

CAERGWRLE

*The Gem of Lovely North Wales*

OFFICIAL GUIDE

# 18. The Ridge of the Grave

The riverside path leading to Cefn y Bedd is quiet and shrouded by thick trees. The tranquillity comes to an end at the bridge over the B5102 Llay road which appears to double as a race track. There must be a by-law here to ensure cars are driven as if Beelzebub himself is hanging off the rear bumper. A tunnel guides the river underneath a huge bridging embankment, atop of which sits the devil's highway. I pause for a second, think of Llandegla and wonder if this would be a more suitable location to bury a small box in the riverbed. A drive over this bridge, lined with trees gives little clue to the deep valley below. It is crossed in seconds, oblivious to the hard toil which made it possible. I contemplate not just this mighty structure, but the many bridges which cross the Alun, from the very first simple wooden affair up near the source, to the historic Packhorse Bridge and the many modern structures. I for one take them for granted; if they weren't where they are, life would be much more difficult, not to say very messy.

The walk previously mentioned in *Hidden Highways of North Wales* returns to Caergwrle via this spot, joining a drover's road as opposed to a packhorse trail. R. J. A. Dutton describes how the route of the road climbed up from a ford which was destroyed when the bridge was constructed. I found the overgrown terrace which carried the road and followed it, as near as was possible, up from the river through holly thickets to where it met the Wat's Dyke path. It continued onward, away from the Alun, its way blazed by a line of trees to Gwastad Farm on the hill.

A smaller older bridge, not as high, stands just downstream from the new one. The view is spectacular from here; the valley floor widens. A Heron flew lazily out of sight under a high watery sky.

I entered Cefn y Bedd; the Ridge of the Grave, and walked the main A541 road onward in the direction of Wrexham past a disused church or chapel half way down the hill which has literally lost its identity. The face of the soft stone block once bearing its name has been worn back to reveal the original layers of strata as they were laid down. The building sits on top of a steep cliff above the Cegidog. I wonder if this is the ridge of the grave, as there are several to choose from in this area. At the bottom of the hill the builder's merchants, where several decades ago I bought supplies to renovate my first house, is broken-glass empty. The Cegidog, which I confess I've never noticed here, runs under the road into the Alun. This is the largest tributary of the Alun, a look at the map shows its origin near Rhydtalog; not so far from that of the Alun, but it takes a far less fussy route. Its junction with the Alun is overgrown, forgotten, out of sight. This is quite depressing; what clearly is a beautiful natural feature is neglected. There are hub caps, traffic cones and fast food containers; no prizes for guessing from which outlet they originated. There must be coded messages in them only visible to litter bugs which say: "Eat contents; drop-kick packaging". I attempted to get to the confluence, but a broken sewerage pipe proved a final insurmountable barrier.

The rivers could be the main focus of the village, there could be riverside cafes and shops where on a Sunday afternoon grandparents could promenade with gurgling bambinos. As it is, a nearby hostelry has long since had last orders called, a post box built into a wall is far enough away from any post office as to constitute a day out for some elderly folk.

There are none of the info boards I've seen in pretty much every other village on the Alun. The name of the village itself screams out for an explanation to passers-by and the curious; at least I can firmly rule out the 'seven in a bed' translation...

The Llay Hall industrial estate straddles the Alun at the south end of Cefn y Bedd, housing all manner of industrial and commercial units. In the past there were iron and wire works, coal mines and brickworks in this area. A mill at this point handled clay, a new addition to the types of material worked by mills powered by the Alun. The colliery operated here from 1873 to 1949 and provided employment for many hundreds, although, as is the nature of the work, fatal accidents were not unknown. The area is peppered with other collieries; if a section were taken through the ground underfoot, it would, no doubt, resemble a big gorgonzola.

The now green spoil heaps of Llay Hall colliery roll into Alyn Waters Country Park. During the sixteenth century the park was part of the large country estate of Gwersyllt Hall, home of the royalist Colonel Robinson who was nearly hanged here. He escaped to France, returning in 1645 to find his house sacked. The hall was demolished in 1910 as a result of mining subsidence. The park was quarried on both sides of the Alun for sand and gravel. If memory serves me correctly, it was later used as a municipal tip. It's been tidied up a lot since then.

Overnight rain had washed away most of the snow; a few dirty mounds and shaded slippery stretches remained, ready to catch out the unsuspecting. It felt warmer than it had for weeks. The river was noisy, in spate, wild. The bank had collapsed in several areas exposing twisted tree trunks and fresh loamy soil. It would have been a bad day to fall in.

At a delicious bend in the river, fragments of stonework could just be seen, projecting out from the wild, tumbling, brown melt water. On quieter days here, the remains of a substantial weir, a large stonework island, sits amphitheatre-like squat in the middle of the river, as if waiting a troupe of actors to be ferried there to perform. The tumbling waters on the eastern side would have served a leat,

still visible, along with the sluice gate. This would have fed Bradley Mill some 300m downstream, where a two-wheeled mill ground corn. It succumbed to that scourge of mills, fire, when it burnt down in 1966.

Further downstream, the swollen river partially covered a wooden walkway which usually traverses a marshy area.

A springtime walk at Alun Waters is highly recommended, hawthorns burst like fireworks with white and pink blossom, willow catkins carpet the floor, and the air is full of tree pollen. On the yellow butter-cupped grassy knoll, skylarks sing their hearts out as they perform vertical take-offs. The waters gently gurgle their way downstream, satisfying a primeval subconscious need for our very life stuff.

*Alun Waters Country Park*

# 19. Wilderness Valley – Shangri-La

*"Walk as if you are kissing the Earth with your feet."*

Thích Nhất Hạnh

A check of the map for the next point at which the Alun could be rejoined revealed a footpath leading off a lane from the Llay – Wrexham road into Wilderness Valley, the inspiration for this peregrination. I saw signs proclaiming "no access", "no footpath", etc. The footpath definitely exists however; it descends through a small collection of old houses with a commune feel about them where we were met by cheery "Hellos!" from people doing Sunday afternoon stuff, washing cars, titivating their gardens. Signs can be misleading.

The path continues alongside a small stream into the secret pocket that is Wilderness Valley. The Alun hugs the contours of the finger-like hill promontory of Bryn Alyn. Here it reaches its southernmost point, the steep-sided slopes of Wilderness Wood bouncing it back north: a full on, 180 degree about-turn.

Bryn Alyn is topped by an Iron Age hill fort. This natural feature would have been incorporated into Wat's Dyke, which enters through the wood from the south. The steep slopes are ringed by the Alun forming a natural moat to the "castle".

The path passes by the ruins of Gwersyllt Corn Mill. The Wilderness Valley area, now quiet, was once a hotbed of milling, powered by the Alun. Other mills have been demolished: Bradley Fulling Mill was engaged in processing cloth, while metal was produced at Bradley Wire Mill. Further downstream Wilderness Mill ground corn.

A footbridge crosses the free-flowing Alun. The river here is fast and wide, un-channelled, choosing its own path. Gravel spits form around gnarled crack willow. Dippers bob and flirt in front of us; they indicate good water quality, feeding on insects on the river bed which need well-oxygenated water. Their presence here is particularly apt and very welcome, as they are sometimes compared to the canaries used in coal mines to show the air is pure. In the days of coal mining in this area, the

Alun was said to have run black.

Improvised farm trailers in the fields give a frontier feel. As on our last visit, we don't see a soul. A cluster of houses stands near the old Wilderness Mill and bridge. Some are new but in keeping with the rustic feel of the valley. The Alun white waters its way through the old sluices.

The eastern slope is towered over by old colliery spoil, while the lane which formerly led to Gresford is rudely truncated by the tree-shrouded Wrexham bypass, completing the isolation of this so near yet so distant-feeling valley. A drive along the adjacent new Llay sky-road seems to iron out the map contours; the Alun flows quietly below, dipping its toe barely noticed into Wrexham's suburbs, invisible from the slope-defying highways.

At Pont Ty Capel we saw no chapel but graffiti going back to 1911. Quality graffiti this, laboriously chipped away into the stone. The themes haven't changed, though: youths marking their territory and proclaiming their love.

The spoil heap had a white dusting of snow. A possible plan to use it as a ski slope could in the future see it fulfil its wintery ambitions.

The wilderness continued along a rough path. No new footprints were visible on the previous day's snow. The riverbank had collapsed in several places, throwing birch trees whole into the flow, which was almost blocked at one point. A fresh vertical bank had been created, large pebbles sticking out, a possible site for kingfishers to nest. Again I had a feeling of Alaskan wilderness, complete with snow on the ground. In some places red tree roots were exposed, like knitting wool or the red weed from War of the Worlds. The Wrexham bypass is very close by, but remains unseen on the other side of the hill. It was cold in the shelter of the trees; thankfully I'd remembered my gloves. The fallen trees and surging river gave this area a remote feel. There must be some of those animals which I'm not going to name here, surely? I'm not the most observant of people, I come to the conclusion my biggest hope of seeing one of them is to spend the maximum amount of time at the river and hope one falls across my line of vision.

The river here seemed to swell and shrink, in some areas a mighty white water flow through grey tombstone rocks; in

others a channelled meander under unstable banks. I kept my distance to avoid making a closer inspection.

A high concrete bridge carries the new Llay – Gresford road across the valley. Spray-painted graphic graffiti this time; it's not 1911 anymore. Gresford Mill, a substantial three storey corn mill was demolished and lies buried under the embankment of the realigned road.

Nearby an old bridge of three arches, much more sedate, straddles the river, testament to a crossing point long since used. My map showed "Gresford Lo." I wondered what the Lo was short for. I tried to apply logic to the location, its geography and history and came up with

Gresford lower crossing. A few days later while driving along the road from Llay I saw "Gresford Lodge" on a gate post nearby; nothing to do with a lower crossing. A grand house of the same name, dating back to around 1790 and much admired once stood here. The elevation facing the Alun had a projecting semi-circular central section with Doric supporting columns. She was demolished in 1956, another victim of subsidence from coal mining, being situated above the Llay main workings.

I pondered a while on the names of Gresford and Marford villages. The ford is clear but Gres and Mar? Gresford is not far

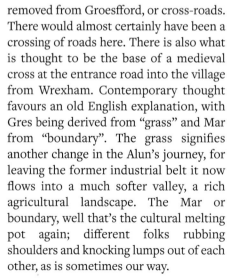

1. *Placid Alun; 2. Angry Alun*

removed from Groesfford, or cross-roads. There would almost certainly have been a crossing of roads here. There is also what is thought to be the base of a medieval cross at the entrance road into the village from Wrexham. Contemporary thought favours an old English explanation, with Gres being derived from "grass" and Mar from "boundary". The grass signifies another change in the Alun's journey, for leaving the former industrial belt it now flows into a much softer valley, a rich agricultural landscape. The Mar or boundary, well that's the cultural melting pot again; different folks rubbing shoulders and knocking lumps out of each other, as is sometimes our way.

# 20. The Lost Pilgrimage

*"It is no use walking anywhere to preach
unless our walking is our preaching"*
*Francis of Assisi*

George Borrow at the beginning of his
*Wild Wales* writes of walking from Chester
through pleasant meadows before crossing
the "river Allan", then through Marford to
the top of a hill from which the view is
"very fine". He chats to a Waggoner,
breathing his team of horses, who tells him
"there isn't such a place to see the country
from, far and near, as where we stand.
Many come to this place to look about
them." He offers "sixpence to drink"
which the Waggoner accepts: "I shall stop
at Pulford and shall be glad to drink your
health in a jug of ale."

The viewpoint would have been close
to Gresford, though he doesn't mention
the church, which I'm sure would have
interested him greatly. If he'd visited a
couple of centuries earlier, I'm sure he'd
have filled a chapter about her.

Before undertaking this walk I'd heard
of Gresford church and its bells and of
course the Gresford colliery disaster, but
I'd never actually been to Gresford. The
A484 Wrexham by-pass takes traffic away
from the village, so unless a deliberate
decision is made to go there, it won't be
chanced upon. Our acquaintance was long
overdue, so up the steep, steep hill from
the Alun did I make my way.

The castellated nave of the church was
first to come into view, followed by the
impressive pinnacled tower that appeared
from behind the Griffin Inn. From this
angle the church dominated the village
green, where stocks would have once
stood. All Saints is big, very big, for a
village. It has been called the finest parish
church in Wales and its bells are one of
The church is built of light brown Cefn
sandstone, which gives it a warm
welcoming colour, but a softness that
suffers from erosion, which must be a
constant battle for its carers. The massive
tower was bathed in warm sunlight from
the west.

There is an ancient yew tree in the
churchyard, near to the east gate entrance
from the village, and it doesn't disappoint.
A central wizened, knobbled and generally

*One of the seven wonders of Wales*

medieval church. It is likely that the altar and yews had formed a sacred site pre-dating even this ancient tree.

A solid comfortable bench near the tower sits under one of the more juvenile yews which encircle the church. I sat for a while, enjoying the sun's warm rays before making a second circuit.

The impressive size of the building is complemented by the fine detail of its gargoyles. Some are at quite low levels which allow them to be fully appreciated; others stare down menacingly, wall-papered against a heavenly blue sky. There are the usual heads of noblemen and saints along with devilish beasts, but there are also lots of scampering animals, world-weary faces, puffed-cheek wind-blowing cherubs, and Wallace and Grommet-like face-pullings. Some are eroded and age-stained black.

I turned the handle on the heavy wooden door, walking into light and openness. Bright sunlight flooded in through the south-facing windows; I could see right down to the chancel and chapels at the east end, above me stretched a fantastic wood-panelled roof. To the right of the entrance was a brightly painted window, showing Lazarus being raised

gnarled stubby trunk gives rise to a mass of smaller twisting boughs. The trunk is holed and in areas rotten, there is netting over the larger openings and evidence of heavy pruning but yews cling to life and there is plenty of healthy new growth providing a green and red berry-speckled canopy over the paths. Yews' longevity and ability to grow new trunks from the original root result in associations with immortality, regeneration and renewal. This particular yew is thought to have been planted around 400 AD. Inside the church there is a Roman altar stone which had been used in the building of the

*1. Roman Altar Stone; 2. Gresford Gargoyles*

from the dead. Its light and colour felt modern in an age-old setting.

The ancient stone-carved font had a laminated information sheet on it which was fascinating; until 1452, the priest at Gresford also looked after the chapel of St Leonard in the valley close by. This had been founded by the Normans in 1175, but fell into disuse when All Saints became a great pilgrimage centre. It poses a question that possibly this font came from that chapel when All Saints was completed in 1498.

Quite a thought: as if 1498 weren't history enough, this font could pre-date that by another couple of centuries! What of the chapel of St Leonard in the valley? By now I'd done a finger-tip tour of the valley along countless maps many times and this wasn't ringing any bells. Although the existence of the chapel is documented, its location isn't known.

In a chapel dedicated to the Trevor family (benefactors of Plas Teg fame) is a mural commemorating the Gresford colliery disaster of 1934. It was one of Britain's worst coal-mining catastrophes, claiming the lives of 266 workers. A violent explosion in the early hours of September 22nd was followed by a fire, which, despite valiant attempts by the rescue brigade, could not be brought under control. A decision was made to seal the shaft. Only 11 of the miner's bodies were recovered, compounding an already tragic loss.

It's hard for me, a modern day biro pilot, to comprehend the grim life of a miner at that time. Toiling deep underground, earning their living from their own physical strength in dirt, dust and heat for long hours and low pay, the potential dangers were legion: roof falls, flooding, suffocation, heavy machinery and explosion. Mine owners and investors were keen to recoup their cash, so decisions they made could literally mean life or death for the miners.

The disaster left some 200 widowed women and 800 fatherless children. It's difficult to imagine the effect of loss on this scale on a small community.

The colliery finally closed in 1973. A memorial, made from the wheel from the pit-head winding gear, was erected in 1982. It's located just off the Pandy roundabout on the A483.

The chancel screens and stalls display fine wood carving. The "Misericords" (mercy seats – their shelves provided discreet support for clerics during long services) are particularly fine, having further intricate and sometimes more daring carvings underneath the hinged seats.

The east wall may help to explain this magnificent large church located in a small community. It is known that Gresford church was a destination for pilgrims from the 1300s to the 1500s. It is believed that the church held an object of veneration of great religious significance. History does not record what the object was: maybe the secret is contained within chiselled stonework or a stained-glass window, awaiting a Dan Brown-style revelation, for as medieval man may have not been able to read text, *we* have lost much of the knowledge of how to read a church. In the corner of the Lady Chapel is a carved recess which rests on the head of a green man, a pagan symbol of the countryside and fertility. It now contains a modern statue of the Virgin and Child, but it is thought that this recess may have once held the sacred object which drew the many medieval pilgrims. There is also evidence that a processional way existed behind the altar; a doorway on each side of the altar is thought to have been for a bridge which could have had a wooden

1. *Gresford colliery disaster mural;*
2. *Gresford memorial; 3. Virgin and child above the Green Man*

access stairway in the adjacent chapels. That human traffic-flow arrangements were required gives an idea of the number of pilgrims which must have been visiting. They would have walked down one aisle, crossed over the processional way, where the sacred object may have been moved to allow pilgrims to view, touch or kiss the relic and make an offering, and then exited via the other aisle. This sounds perfectly feasible. I have joined throngs of modern day pilgrims being guided in a similar manner while visiting the relics of St James in Santiago de Compostela.

And so it was for several centuries that Gresford prospered as pilgrims came from near and far to see the now unknown relic, to request miracle cures and make their offerings.

On a Saturday afternoon I spent several hours at All Saints in splendid solitude, save for a woman and child who popped in for a quick prayer. I thought of the numerous times I have joined a scrum of people and shuffled through the great cathedrals of Britain and the Continent, yet here I had it all to myself. It is easy to be drawn in by the size and magnificence of these buildings, easy to be carried along in a tide of humanity and miss the detail, not to say the spirituality of the place, but here I had time aplenty to appreciate intricate wood carvings from the stalls to the roof, the unusual brightly coloured floor tiles in the chancel and the fine chandeliers suspended over the central aisle. This precious space is required as much as it ever was; a sanctuary to wrap its arms around us, an escape from the mind-sense bombardment of modern life, a shelter from the storm. And it's all on our doorstep.

Gresford has eight bells with an approximate weight of 4.7 tonnes, the heaviest single bell being the tenor at 1.2 tonnes. The headstocks, frames, etc, add another best part of a tonne. The whole caboodle has to be secured some 40 feet off the ground in the belfry, in a manner which allows rotation by the ringers on the church floor.

'The finest parish church in Wales'. – I wouldn't argue with that statement.

I wonder what it was that those pilgrims of old venerated; was it a small bodily remain of a saint, or a piece of the true cross which may now sit somewhere hidden gathering dust, unnoticed, its provenance broken?

Who knows, maybe one day the object will be found in a blaze of publicity, and the faithful will be queuing up in All Saints once more. Gresford could be awash with *Peregrinos* on their *Camino*, travelling from far-off places, the village buzzing.

The great pilgrimage era lasted only a small portion of the life of this sacred site. Whatever happens in the future the church is pretty much the same as it was back in those heady days, minus one object. It's a fantastic building, a peaceful sanctuary for contemplation, which can be enjoyed at leisure.

# 21. Telford's Plan and more Treasure

*"...Mr Telford was of the most genial disposition and a delightful companion, his laugh was the heartiest I ever heard; it was a pleasure to be in his society."*

*Telford's assistant recorded in his diary his memories of his deceased employer.*

The river after Gresford emerges from the valley into open farmland. My eyes had to adjust to bright snow-covered fields under clear blue skies. I saw another memorial plaque attached to a tree. The importance in which the Alun is held, and the happiness it can deliver, is clear. The course swept to the Wrexham bypass, leaving only a narrow strip of steep snow-coated bank to traverse. It was, as they say, passable with care. Following this river was like life itself: sometimes the path was well marked and flat, the sun was shining and it was a joy: at other times the way was uncertain, cold, dark, slippery and unclear.

The valley is a corridor, shared by the now dominant A483, the railway line and the placid Alun. It could also have had another bedfellow; a canal running north from Pontcysyllte Aqueduct to Chester and onwards to the Mersey at Ellesmere Port. The section from Chester northwards was indeed built.

In 1791 a proposal was made for a canal which would link the Mersey with the Dee at Chester and the Severn at Shrewsbury to serve the prosperous agricultural district of Shropshire with coal, lime and other goods and to tap the rich coal and iron district around Wrexham, Ruabon and Brymbo.

The canal would have climbed a flight of locks from the north end of Pont Cysyllte and then descend an even greater flight through this valley into the Cheshire plain. Water supply to the short summit level between these two flights was the great problem. Reservoirs were planned in the narrow valleys which run up into the eastern slopes of Ruabon and Eclusham mountains and the cutting of a short feeder canal called the Froode branch was actually begun.

All manner of schemes were considered to negotiate the hills and ensure adequate supplies of water. These physical difficulties, however, coincided with a financial slump, and the end of 'canal mania'. The northern route was abandoned in favour of an altogether different route via Whitchurch and Nantwich so that Pont Cysyllte, Ellesmere, Chester and Ellesmere Port were indeed connected, albeit via an altogether different route.

Had the scheme gone ahead it would, I am sure, have graced this section of the Alun with a solution which would not only been practical but would actually have complemented the countryside that carried it, for the name of the gentleman in charge was one Thomas Telford, the great Victorian engineer. His aqueducts at Chirk and Froncysyllte and the Menai Suspension Bridge are not only engineering feats of the highest order, but works of art too.

The river goes on a long lazy sweep here, the land having lost the majority of its gradient. The sound from the bypass distant to my right was muffled. A fox traversed a flat sheep-grazed field. Too early for lambs, they seemed unflustered. Benches at the riverbank near favoured fishing pegs were too much to resist. I sat down and closed my eyes for a while to drink it in: a compensation for the cold wet feet.

I didn't see any anglers but I could well imagine the pleasure of spending a summer's evening here. A fresh trout would be a bonus. I favour them wrapped in bacon and roasted in the oven – delicious! I scanned the bank for you-know-whats, which would be in direct competition with the anglers here. I visualised fishing here with my stout sea gear – I would have had difficulty not casting straight over to the other side. Some of the pegs seemed to be surrounded by trees and had branches above them. I wondered how on earth a fly could be cast here. Different methods for different waters: there's more ways of killing a pig than just choking it with cream.

A cold blast of icy air reminded me it was winter. I ended my daydream. A heron flew straight down the course of the river.

At the next bench, I gazed over the planted field. Green shoots about four inches high were reaching for the sky. The field was littered with rounded pebbles, some dissected by the blade of a plough.

Approaching Burton, a footbridge crossed the river. A chap clad in combat fatigues, looking like a gamekeeper, walked toward me; as usual, I expected to be

shooed away. Again I was proved wrong; he turned out to be a consultant ecologist looking for dipper nesting sites. We had a knowledge transfer: I advised of dipper sightings and bridges I had passed on the way: he enlightened me on unmentionable animal spotting signs – footprints in soft mud with webs between toes, and mud slides into the river are a giveaway.

In the fields to the left here, the Alun delivered yet another Bronze Age treasure. In 2004, metal detector enthusiasts discovered what has come to be known as "The Burton Hoard" – an exceptional collection of gold jewellery and bronze tools unparalleled anywhere else in the UK. The objects had been carefully placed in a ceramic pot and buried in the ground in what appears to have been another ritual offering near the Alun. The hoard included a gold torc, twisted wire bracelet, necklace pendant, beads and rings. It is a fine example of twisting and soldering techniques by an unknown goldsmith.

The find dates from 1300 to 1350 BC, and is on display at the National Museum of Wales, adjacent to the Caergwrle Bowl. The Alun was clearly highly significant during the Bronze Age. Who knows how many other treasures have been uncovered and dispersed in the intervening three millennia, and how many more remain to be discovered?

The Alun's final major change in direction from north-east to east at Cam-yr-Alyn (Cam translates as step or crooked) brought me to a fantastic and totally unexpected outsized weir. No "weir" is marked on my map, but on closer inspection, the structure is clearly shown and needs no fanfare. I sat and appreciated the continuous stream of white horses. If I had been aware of its existence and size, possibly its effect would have been lessened. Serendipity is a powerful magnifier. A salmon ladder dissected the centre section; I hope it gets plenty of use. A small mill race fed water away, disappearing under ugly bridges before emerging again at the picture postcard Rossett Mill. A fulling mill known as Bellot's Mill once stood at the weir, built in 1572 by a Thomas Bellott, Sheriff of Denbighshire.

## 22. Trouble at Mill

*"Within this thin wafer of bread is caught up symbolically the labor of plow and of sowing, of harvest and threshing, of milling, of packing, of transportation, of financing, of selling and packaging. Man's industrial life is all there."*

*Wilford O. Cross*

Rossett Mill has an inscribed date of 1661. An information board in the village tells of the first mill on this site being built in 1544 and then extended in 1661. "The Spirit of Rossett, Marford and Gresford" by Helen Maurice-Jones, in addition to a collection of great photos of Rossett mills and bridges, gives the mill as originally having been built about 1474 during the reign of King Edward IV.

When it was built, it was classed as a rogue mill. Laws at the time specified set distances for the building of new mills upstream of existing mills so as they didn't have an adverse effect on their water supply. Rossett mill was deemed to be too close to Marford mill and hence "stealing its water supply".

Its survival as a rogue mill wasn't the last threat it faced. It has recently changed hands; the previous to current owner bought the derelict mill in 1973. Soon after, the building of the A483 dual carriageway commenced a short distance away, with a planned route which would have dissected the mill race, depriving it of its water supply. Demolition was a real possibility. At the eleventh hour an agreement was reached, saving the mill and its leat, the mill was restored, its wheel turned again. I hope the mill continues to execute its original purpose, water flowing, turning grain into flour in a way largely unchanged for millennia.

The undershot water wheel is still in place: less efficient than an overshot wheel, it was nonetheless probably installed due to there being little gradient in this area. From the start of her journey high on the slopes of Cyrn-y-Brain which summits at 565m, the Alun has descended to an altitude of around 15m here, expending a huge amount of energy on the way. She has only a few metres further to fall to the Dee. Wagtails flitted about, reflected in the mill pond, which was...flat.

Marford Mill on the opposite side of the road was the original crown mill to which all tied tenants had to send their

*Rossett Mill*

corn. This would have given control over the populace and provided a means of raising taxes. Some early mill leases gave the miller the right to break hand querns used by the hoi polloi to grind their corn tax-free. Death and taxes, those two certainties of life!

Rossett wins on aesthetics and location, Turner must have had similar thoughts for he sketched her in 1794, as a basis for his subsequent watercolour, but Marford outdoes Rossett with its two wheels and greater longevity. The information board shows that a mill was recorded here in the 1086 Domesday Book.

That's a lot of grist to the mill.

As we nosed about (Sion being today's accomplice), looking and failing, to find any evidence for a possible third mill in this area; "Marford Old Mill," a man appeared from the nearby houses and kindly gave us an overview of recent events at the mill, where he has been involved in the restoration.

He regularly turns and greases the bearings of the larger wheel; the smaller wheel has unfortunately seized. Both have been reconstructed to a high standard. He pointed out the wooden sections, reconstructed from carefully sourced materials and their attachment brackets, hand-made by a local blacksmith. Internally, only the gear wheels of the original milling accoutrements are still in place. In the past he has seen certain furred aquatic mammals playing on the grassed area nearby, though none recently and has also seen salmon and sea trout below the weir at Cam-yr-Alyn.

The Welsh Mills Society kindly passed on a list of 32 mills which have existed on the Alun, based on Ordnance Survey maps of 1872, 1899 and 1912. These are shown in the table to which I have added 3 others which have come to my attention (numbers 11, 34 and 35.). A further 7 mills were listed on its tributaries.

Alun power was put to a wide range of uses:

Its first and main use was for milling corn to produce various sifted grains such as white flour, bran and animal feed.

Its industrial uses included the manufacture of paper, rope and wire, the working of clay, lead ore and timber, and the powering of foundry machinery. The grinding of silica stone and cloth fulling were also undertaken.

Several mills were adapted to generate electricity. The biggest source of power to be harnessed from the Alun's waters might paradoxically not be on the Alun at all.

*Marford Mill*

## Mills on the River Alun

| | Name | Type | Fate |
|---|---|---|---|
| 1 | Llandegla Mill | Corn | Demolished 1950s |
| 2 | Creigiog Mill | Corn | Private house |
| 3 | Llanarmon Mill | Corn | Private house |
| 4 | Maes-y-hafn Lead Works | Lead | Derelict |
| 5 | Llanferres Mill | Corn | Private house |
| 6 | Pentre Mill, Loggerheads | Corn/Saw | Open for viewing within Loggerheads Country Park |
| 7 | Glanalyn Mine 1 | Lead | The larger wheelpit remains |
| 8 | Glanalyn Mine 2 | | |
| 9 | Unnamed lead mine | Lead | Fed by The Great Leete, 3,200m. |
| 10 | Nant Alyn Flour Mill | Lead/Corn | Private House/Caravan Park Office |
| 11 | *'Rolling Mill'* | | *Local term, mill directly on the river, large stones remain, moved by floods.* |
| 12 | Rhydymwyn Flour Mill | Corn | Demolished 1966 |
| 13 | Rhydymwyn Foundry | Metal/Saw | On former Valley works site. |
| 14 | Alyn Tinplate Works | Metal | Mold Cotton Mill on site 1792-1866; tinplate factory built 1878; now Dynea. |
| 15 | Alyn Mills | Corn | Demolished? |
| 16 | Leadmills | Place name | Mold – Queensferry road crosses river Alyn |
| 17 | Pentre Mill | Corn | Private house |
| 18 | Pont-bleiddyn Mill | Corn | Demolished |
| 19 | Caergwrle Saw Mills | Saw | Ceased operations c1928. |
| 20 | Caergwrle (Bookers) Mill | Corn/Power | Rebuilt 1852; later provided electricity. Now a private house |
| 21 | Hope Mills | Paper | Demolished |

| 22 | Unnamed | ? | Llay Hall Colliery workshops area (Upstream) |
|---|---|---|---|
| 23 | North Wales Coal, Iron and Brick Co | Clay | Llay Hall Colliery workshops area (Downstream) |
| 24 | Bradley Mill | Corn | Two wheels; burned 1966. |
| 25 | Bradley Fulling Mill | Fulling | Demolished. |
| 26 | Bradley Wire Mill | Metal | Demolished. |
| 27 | Gwersyllt Mill | Corn | Ruined; two millstones on site in 2000. |
| 28 | Wilderness Mill | Corn | Demolished by 1899. |
| 29 | Gresford Mill | Corn | Demolished for road diversion. |
| 30 | Bellott's Mill, Rossett | Fulling | Demolished. |
| 31 | Rossett Mill | Corn | Restored |
| 32 | Marford Mill | Corn | Two wheels – tail water from Rossett Mill. Now headquarters of BASC |
| 33 | Marford Old Mill | Corn | Demolished |
| 34 | *Horsley Estate Mill* | *Corn?* | *Recorded in 1272, demolished.* |
| 35 | *Ithel's Bridge* | *Corn?* | |

With thanks to The Welsh Mills Society for information supplied.

There is a proposal to install a hydro-electric plant at the outfall of the Milwr Tunnel. The man-made feature which has had the biggest effect on the Alun could yet utilise its pilfered gains for the common good.

The bridge in front of Rossett Mill carrying the main road to the Chester – Wrexham bypass road was built in 1921: just about everything seems to be date-marked in Rossett; very useful if, say, you were writing a book. A pillar from an old bridge stands forlorn in the Alun; no date on this. Shops and houses near the Alun have high doorsteps, possibly a defence against flooding. Rossett suffered badly in the floods of 2000. A path led from the bridge along the Alun; snowdrops tentatively peeked out at its edges.

*The Alyn pub at Rossett (tough research)*

# 23. The End

As Sophia and I left Rossett on a January Sunday on a cold, clear blue-skied morning, the Alun was not as wide as I had anticipated it would be here, but it did have a fair depth. We walked along the tree-lined riverbank; my thoughts once again turned to the no-name animal and how I was rapidly running out of river in which to see one. At Cook's Bridge, a Grade II listed single-span sandstone construction; an angler had set up on the opposite bank for a chilly session. The next bridge is more modern with a large concrete span. I saw tracks in the soft mud and learnt that a young man of this parish, and who shall remain nameless, like my animal friends, was apparently, in the considered opinion of another, "a shit".

The ground under foot was frozen hard; in addition to a vanguard robin and the other usual suspects, long-tailed tits, lapwing and fieldfare were our companions. There are some delicious bends in the river at Ithells Bridge Farm. This location was idyllic, the sun bathing the garden in warming light, a bench inviting a rest and contemplation. This was the location of the last corn mill to use the Alun's services before she reached the Dee.

The final stretch to the Dee was, to be honest, disappointing. High banks, understandably in this truly flat flood plain, sped the river in a tamed, controlled, almost drainage ditch fashion to the Dee. Any interesting little bends which may have existed in this most meandering of rivers had long since been straightened out. The river had obviously been higher; a high tide mark was visible about eight feet above the flow. Stranded litter hung from trees, whose trunks and branches were coated in dreary brown-grey mud.

In the dreamy recesses of my mind I had visualised this stretch to be the widest, with slow meanders under leafy oaks inviting moonlit skinny dipping. Well, it was below freezing and I kept my pants firmly on. To be fair, a tranquil summer evening down here would most likely be an altogether different affair.

The ultimate short stretch was a further anti-climax; the path veered off away from the flow, which was hidden in a thicket of undergrowth, behind a barbed wire fence.

The brave little Alun flowed silently through this high security landscape into the majestic Dee, a mere tributary, one of many – out of sight and unsung. Holiday chalets were all around, some on stilts, prepared for floods. Many looked inviting, a nice place to spend slow summer days, but others look like the kind of places where villains could hole up undetected, torturing themselves with daytime television.

We set up our frosty picnic, looked over the spot where the Alun ended, subsumed by the Dee, over to England on the opposite side bank, and toasted our journey with warming coffee.

The river Dee, afon Dyfrdwy – the 'holy one', 'river of divine waters'; the meandering one meets the divine one. The Romans, who knew a thing or two about god's, adapted the Celtic name to Deva for their fortress on her banks at Chester.

It's often said that it's better to travel than to arrive; in the case of the Alun for me this was true. I had a sense of completion, tinged with the realisation that its final stage, tamed and compliant, had been a little disappointing. My mind drifted back; it seemed like an age since I was strolling along the wild unfettered river at Llandegla and Llanarmon. Still, the Alun has a bigger part to play, feeding the Dee onward to Liverpool Bay.

When I got home, I checked how far I'd walked; I laid out the maps covering the Alun's life from birth to end on my living room floor. It once again lived up to its name, in that three maps were required to complete the task – one of them twice as it inked its way south to north along the left side then reappeared travelling north to south along the right side.

I completed the journey a second time, this time following its route with a map measuring wheel. When I'd taken the two different scales of the maps used into account, I arrived at a smidgen under 40 km or about 25 miles in real money. It was impossible to follow all the twists and turns accurately with the wheel of the measuring device, but I was quite surprised: my feet insisted it was longer.

Traversed by some 78 bridges, once powering 35 known mills, guarded by at least five forts/castles, neighbour to countless churches and religious sites, finding place of at least three treasures of national significance, falling some 550 metres on its way, the Alun was quite a journey.

Mark Twain wrote that when he had 'mastered the language' of the Mississippi and had come to know 'every trifling feature' in his days as a steamboat pilot, he 'lost something which could not be restored to him as long as he lived. All the grace, the beauty, the poetry had gone out of the majestic river, all the value any feature of it had was the amount of usefulness it could furnish toward safe piloting'. I'm lucky in that the Alun is my companion purely for pleasure, all her graceful curves, reflected images and quiet stretches will, hopefully, beguile me for years to come.

# 24. Watershed

On an April day, between deluges rather than showers, events conspired to bring me to the campsite at Llandegla on the banks of the Alun. Maybe I'd watched too many documentaries; maybe I just had too much time on my hands, but for whatever reason, my previous idea of where the Alun began had been just too hazy.

On arrival I had asked the owner if she knew where the source lay. She wasn't sure. She gave the names of farms located further upstream where I could make enquiries. She also confirmed my earlier assumption that the stream joining from the east at this point was not the Alun and further informed that this was known locally as the 'Alun Bach.' I like this. The Nile has the Blue and the White; the Alun has the Bach, and by default, the Mawr. I liked even more my pitch right next to their confluence.

I headed south; to the start of the footpath I had previously followed which lay a few hundred yards along the racetrack identified on the map as the A5104.

I followed the lively, effervescent, "juve-Nile", if you will, Alun upstream as it twisted, turned, leaped about and generally enjoyed itself in the unadulterated headwaters.

At each confluence of streams, I selected the larger of the two and continued. This wasn't always a quick decision; sometimes they were indistinguishable in volume. In these instances I would spend several minutes flicking my eyes between the two before selecting the one with the greater *rate* of flow.

I needed to repeat this process several times as I progressed up the valley, but even so, the flow seemed to defy logic, in

*1. The First Bridge; 2. The Mother Valley;
3. The first meander of the Alun*

that, in several areas it seemed to shrink away, fooling me into thinking the source was near, before seemingly swelling again further upstream.

At a sheepfold near the A542, the unidentified flow which joined almost at a right angle coming off the hills to my left was definitely the greater, so it was time to leave the valley floor and head uphill. The stream further up the valley was shown on my map as a thin wiry blue line and was identified as the '*afon Morwynion*' (river of Maidens). This puzzled me slightly, as it appeared much longer than the section I was about to follow, so logically was the

Alun? Streets sometimes change name along their length, but a length of river doesn't generally change name.

*Footnote:*

On another day, accompanied by Sion, we followed the lesser flow, up through a boggy morass sliced with drainage channels. At a rectangular stand of trees the flow reduced to the slightest of trickles. We walked the fenced perimeter of the fir trees, at the opposite diagonal the corresponding trickle flowed *away* from Llandegla – the arboreal cover concealed the watershed between the Alun and the Morwynion. The map shows a straight blue line connecting the two trickles; this must be a drainage ditch, which I had misinterpreted as a continuation of the Alun. The contours on the map confirm the watershed. A 280m stubby fingered contour line points toward Llandegla from the Morwynion, while the tight contours of Cyrn y Brain, fall down to an equally lazy 280m line on the Alun side. The Morwynion runs south west into the Dee at Carrog, the two flows head off 180 degrees apart, to be re-united downstream of Holt.

The flow through a concrete culvert below the road confirmed my choice. It sped the water on its way in a true straight line, a solid walled indication of its volume, which was obviously greater here than how it appeared to be hundreds of metres earlier in its boggy and porous, soft-walled confines which were difficult to define. The course ran parallel to the road before twisting to the east and back underneath it near Pentre Bwlch.

A footpath nearby took me to a knoll opposite the ruins of an old dwelling. With bracken around me and heavy peat soil underfoot, the wind picked up and a few spots of rain liberated themselves from the ominous black clouds ahead. This was the uplands proper. It had to be the mother valley, this was the final summit, there was nowhere she could hide now; the Alun had to rise from the slopes ahead of me.

I passed two sheep carcasses, then the remains of a crow; a tough landscape. Waterlogged moss underfoot was heavy going, I followed sheep tracks but they were invariably cul de sacs, as they offered the least resistance for water flowing down which made it slippery for creatures such as I, going up. I was wearing wellingtons which were ideal for the valley floor, but not so good on upland slopes. They were steel toe-capped, for that extra bit of discomfort, my own Kailash factor. I trudged through bilberry and bracken, arriving at a footbridge carrying a right of way, the first of the many bridges over the Alun. A very stout affair made of old sleepers, unexpected way up here. The flow seemed to diminish slightly at a plateau where it divided into channels, a kind of diminutive delta section. It was tricky to cross; some of them were really deep. I saw mini-jacuzzis of bubbles, evidence of springs. Possibly in drier weather this would be the start point: not on this day, as the land rose upward to the mast of a wireless station high above. I could see numerous tanks and vessels on the slopes, fed by pipes which collected water for the drier times ahead. Onwards and upwards I went, eventually arriving at a natural amphitheatre where the headwaters rise. This acted as a collection point for water percolating down though the heather and mosses above. The origin at last!

### Quest over!

Should I have fallen to my knees in thanks for safe passage to this spot?

In the end, I decided a sprinkling of the cool pure water on my sweating forehead was sufficient. Smoke black clouds billowed over the summit, almost close enough to touch; there was a steady drip of rainfall. I was a long way from the campsite but I reckoned that I'd earned a rest, a chance to reflect and take in the magnificent views. It wasn't as if I was ever going to find myself in that spot again. I could see the Ponderosa Cafe way below, its doors closed, and the high pitched Bizzy Bee motorbikes having returned to their hives. I wondered how many people had been here: farmers certainly, but I wondered if any other curious soul had had the urge to follow the Alun until it is no more.

I went over the facts. I'd followed the greatest flow at each confluence to arrive at this spot. I wondered if another wandering dreamer were to carry out their own search for the source, and a localised downpour on the opposite side of the valley could skew the flow leading them to 'Nant Cae Mawr' (Stream of the Big Field), then they would reach a different conclusion to mine. There would, however, be a contradiction with the nomenclature on their map and they could, if sufficiently driven, take issue with Ordnance Survey on this point. Alternatively they could come to the same conclusion as I originally had at the outset of my journey and call the whole area above Llandegla 'headwaters' and repair to the Crown for a pint.

I returned to the campsite via Cyrn-y-Brain, after a time-consuming, energy-sapping, yet blissful wrong turn through Llandegla Forest. I lay on by my back next to a campfire, gazed up at the ceiling of Satish Kumar's 'million star hotel'; and listened to the two Alun's getting to know each other. I cracked open a bottle of beer, toasted serendipity and sank into an enormous face-consuming smile, in a state of perfect peace...

# 25. Macbeth

*"Success consists of going from failure to failure without loss of enthusiasm"*
*Winston Churchill*

It was colder than I had expected, so I had to scrape the ice off my windscreen before heading off on an early morning jaunt in search of mad march hares. I picked an area close to the Alun of course; I can't seem to let her go. The previous few days had been almost identical, in that a cold misty morning soon cleared to reveal blue skies. Those days had been spent in work, only catching glimpses of sky between windowless buildings. The weekend was not as accommodating; the cold mist stubbornly hung on. I skirted the fields, scouring the edges through binoculars in search of hares. A great spotted woodpecker close by provided a welcome diversion, drilling away on an old crack willow. Of Hares there was no sign; I'd picked this walk on a whim rather than on sound reasoning. My path had periodically coincided with the Alun. Ducks and wood pigeons had provided an early warning system for any more interesting flora on the banks.

The woodpecker was no longer in earshot, and there appeared to be no other wildlife to beguile me as I strolled to a suitable point to rest before heading back feeling slightly melancholic. I blamed a splash behind me on noisy ducks, but then I heard one stone rocking upon another. I turned, expecting to see a dog down by the river accompanied by a stealthy walker. It was nothing so mundane, for staring right at me was an otter. For a moment I froze. In an instant it was into the water and away. A few steps downstream I saw it re-emerge on the opposite bank for several seconds only before it slinked back under water. It made one more appearance on a gravel spit some twenty feet upstream. In a thrice he was back in the river and gone, leaving only an oily looking swirl on the surface. I scanned the river both ways but there was no sign. He must have been visible for a maximum of thirty seconds. I walked briskly upstream, short-cutting bends in the hope of catching him up, all the while saying to myself "I've seen an otter," occasionally varying my mantra to "an otter I have seen." The curse was over.

Macbeth, Macbeth, Macbeth!

After several years of unsuccessful scouring of the Alun, day and night (night being particularly difficult on account of the darkness), I popped out in search of march hares and here, in broad daylight an otter announced its presence to me, not once, but twice. Thank you, Mr or Mrs Otter; thank you. I searched for another half hour but to no avail. Not even any watery footprints on the banks.

The otter (dwr-ci, literally water-dog, or alternatively dyfrgi); it was such a privilege to see one in the wild. Evidence from Iron Age excavations shows otters were not a food source, indicating they may have been held sacred, a link between two worlds, life and death. For me, after years of searching, it certainly felt like a spiritual experience. Let's hope their numbers increase so that this feeling can be oft repeated.

The Alun is a perpetual story, constantly changing, continually having her secrets revealed. New chapters could be added, pages tweaked for time-circular eternities. Who knows: maybe even the Gold Cape may one day be eclipsed by some new dazzling find. For now the scribbling can cease, and the pencils parked up.

I will continue to walk the Alun as long as I can. I'm sure she has many more treats in store for me. I have a remaining wish of seeing a water vole on the Alun, but I wouldn't mind if that wish takes a while to fulfil...so that I can just keep on looking.

# Bibliography

Borrow, George: (1928) *Wild Wales*, T. Nelson and Sons, Ltd. London and Edinburgh

Brown, Ian: (2004) *Discovering a Welsh Landscape*, Windgather Press Ltd. Macclesfield

Cleveley, Vic: (2000) *Mills on the River Alyn*, Melin 16, Journal of the Welsh Mills Society, Ceredigion

Dodd, Quentin RH: (2012) *Plas yn Mhowys and the Flintshire cannel Oil Industry*, Ystrad Alun 12, Mold and District Civic Society

Dutton, R. J. A.: (1997) *Hidden Highways of North Wales*, Gordon Emery, Chester

Ebbs, Cris: (1993) *The Milwr Tunnel*, Cris Ebbs, Llanferres

Friends of Rhydymwyn Valley, *A Tale of Two Villages, Rhydymwyn and Hendre*

Hope and Caergwrle Heritage Trail Committee: (2002), edited by David Healey, *Hope and Caergwrle*, Bridge Books. Wrexham

Irving Washington: (1820) 'The Angler', part of *The Sketch Book of Geoffrey Crayon Gent*, G. P. Putnam's Sons, New York

Jones, J. Colin: (1995), *Gresford village and church and Royal Marford*, Privately published

Kirk, David: (1998), *A tour in Wales* by Thomas Pennant, abridged version, Gwasg Carreg Gwalch, Llanrwst

Lewis, Pete: (2008), *Wat's Dyke Heritage Trail*, Alyn Books, Cilcain

Llandegla Millenium Action Group: (2003) *Llandegla (Droving) Llandegla then and now*

MacGregor Neil: *A History of the World in 100 Objects*, Penguin, BBC/British Museum

Maurice-Jones, Helen: (2003), T*he Spirit of Rossett, Marford & Gresford*, Landmark Publishing Ltd., Ashbourne

Phoenix, Rhona and Matthews, Alison: (2006), *A History of Hope and Caergwrle*, Bridge Books, Wrexham

Pritchard, T. W.: (2009), *St Winefride, her Holy Well and the Jesuit Mission*, c.650-1930', Bridge Books, Wrexham

Rolt, L. T. C.: (2007), *Thomas Telford*, Sutton Publishing Limited, Stroud

Williams, C. J.: (1987), T*he Lead Mines of the Alyn Valley*, Flintshire Historical Society Journal Vol 29. Hawarden

With thanks to Denbighshire and Flintshire County Councils for their information boards and The Welsh Mills Society for information provided.